LANGUAGE IN PAPUA NEW GUINEA

LANGUAGE IN PAPUA NEW GUINEA

Edited by
Toru Okamura

HITUZI SYOBO PUBLISHING
TOKYO
2007

Contents

Contributors vi
Preface vii
Acknowledgements ix
Maps x

1 Coordinate Constructions in Kewapi: A Papuan Language of the Southern Highlands of Papua New Guinea 1
   Apoi Yarapea

2 Preservation of Endangered Languages: Issues and Problems 33
   Ruth Saovana-Spriggs

3 The Role of Lingua Francas in Papua New Guinea 55
   Daniel K. Leke

4 On the Degree of Contact Language Stabilization: A Contrastive Study of Tok Pisin and Nauruan Pidgin 77
   Toru Okamura

5 The German Language in Papua New Guinea 107
   Craig Alan Volker

6 Notes on Japanese Language Teaching in Papua New Guinea 127
   Yasunori Kawazumi

Index 137

Contributors

APOI YARAPEA
Department of Language and Communication,
PNG University of Technology,
Papua New Guinea

RUTH SAOVANA-SPRIGGS
Department of Political and Social Change, RSPAS,
Australian National University,
Australia

DANIEL K. LEKE
Department of English Communication,
University of Papua New Guinea,
Papua New Guinea

TORU OKAMURA
Department of Intercultural Studies,
Tezukayama Gakuin University,
Japan

CRAIG ALAN VOLKER
Department of Foreign Studies,
Gifu Shotoku Gakuen University,
Japan

YASUNORI KAWAZUMI
Department of Language and Literature,
University of Goroka,
Papua New Guinea

Preface

Research on the languages of Papua New Guinea often fails to grasp the views of New Guinean linguists. Many European linguists contributed to the understanding of New Guinean languages. It would take a page to list the contributors. It is important that we encourage and tolerate language studies by the New Guineans in the 21st century. What seems to be lacking, however, is New Guineans' views on language.

Japan provides an illuminating example. At the end of 19th century, Japan tried to learn Western cultures positively because they were regarded as Japan's goal in modernization. They acquired aspects of Western culture such as medicine and physics, but at the same time overlooked their own traditional values. Japanese linguists, for example, considered that Western languages are better than Japanese. Due to the socio-historical background then, it could not be helped.

Such circumstances delayed the study of Japanese by homegrown linguists. Furthermore, they analyzed the Japanese language using Western methods. A Western approach does apply to Western languages, but not to Japanese. Japan today is entirely different. Over the past few decades a considerable number of studies have been made on the language by Japanese linguists. Recent studies of Japanese language and culture have been widely publicized abroad. Also the Japanese are now very proud of accepting different cultures, not just imitating very flexibly as they did in their past.

Fortunately some young and talented linguists are from Papua New Guinea. Dr Apoi Yarapea from the PNG University of Technology, Ruth Saovana-Spriggs from the Australian National University and Daniel Leke from the University of Papua new Guinea for example are very active in linguistics. Dr Craig Alan Volker is now a Professor of linguistics at Gifu Shotoku Gakuen University in Japan.

Their studies of Papua New Guinean languages have affected linguists all over the world.

Some other Papua New Guinean linguists could also contribute to the book in the future. This is very important to us. This book will advance linguistics studies in Papua New Guinea. In other words, we could say it is a turning point.

Toru Okamura

Acknowledgements

I am indebted to Craig Alan Volker (Gifu Shotoku Gakuen University) for his help in planning of this volume. Thanks to his support, I was able to finish it as easily. I also received much useful advice and encouragement from Dicks Thomas and Yasunori Kawazumi during the preparations. I should also like to give thanks for a great deal of secretarial assistance from Ms Naoko Eda, the Faculty of Literature, Tezukayama Gakuin University, while preparing this book. This research was supported in part by a grant from Tezukayama Gakuin University.
Many linguists from Papua New Guinea could play a part in the writing of the book some day-in particular, to Philip Tama, Robert Baraka, Kenneth Sumbuk, F. Pat and Helen Vetunawa. Many thanks to all the staff members at Hituzi Syobo Publishing for undertaking this project.

I would like to dedicate the book to my father Masatatsu Okamura and my mother Kaneko Okamura, who shared a worried interest in this project but who both passed away before its publication.

Toru Okamura

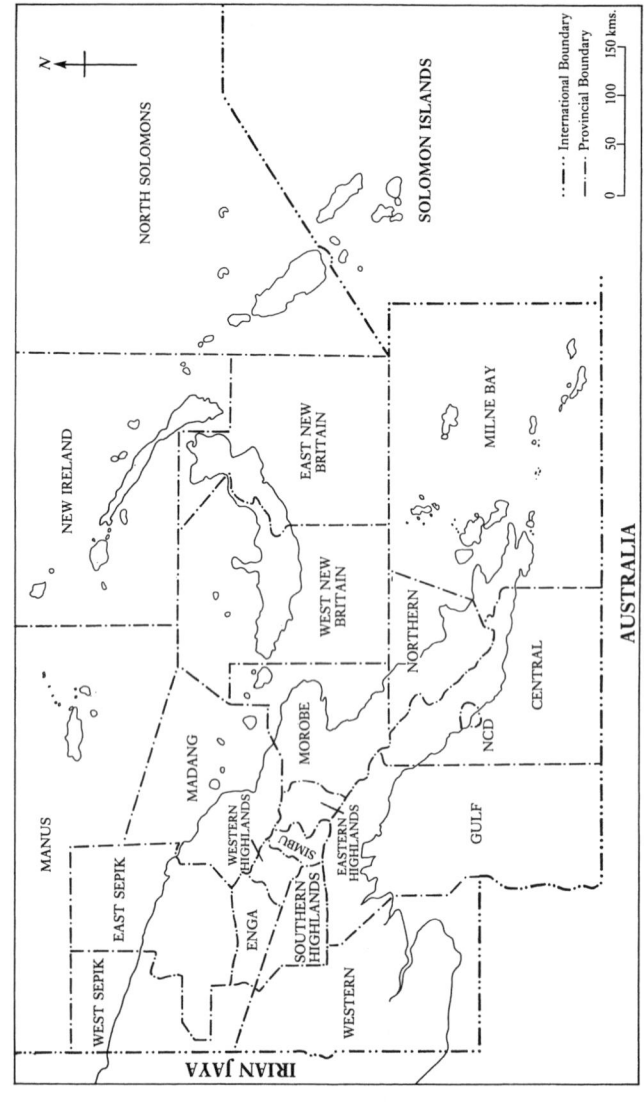

Provinces of Papua New Guinea (from Wheeler and Everist in Romaine 1992: 16)

Coordinate Constructions and Switch Reference in Kewapi: A Papuan Language of the Southern Highlands of Papua New Guinea [1]

Apoi Yarapea
Papua New Guinea University of Technology

1. Introduction

This chapter outlines coordinate constructions in Kewapi. Coordinate structures are categorized as coordinate independent and dependent types in section 3. Section 2 is a sketch of Kewapi typology.

2. A sketch of Kewapi

Kewapi, a Papuan language of Papua New Guinea, shares some of the general morphosyntactic features of the larger Trans New Guinea (TNG) family.

The phonological systems of TNG languages are generally fairly simple (Foley 1986). Segmental phonemes show a dominance of central vowels (Foley 2000) in a system of usually five vowels /i, e, a, o, u/ (Wurm 1982, Foley 1986). Fricatives are rare – often one fricative (Wurm 1982: 77) and the basic consonants are /p, m, w, t, s, n, y, k, ʔ/ (Foley 1986: 55). The proto consonants of the Engan family, which includes Kewapi, are: /p, k, b, g, f, s, g, m, n/ and vowels are: /i, u, e, o, ə, a/ (Franklin 2001: 145). Kewapi has six vowels /i, e, ə, a, o, u/ and fifteen consonants /b, m, p, w, t, d, n, s, l, r, c, ñ, y, g, k/. Of the fifteen consonants three are fricatives: /p/, /s/ and

/k/. On suprasegmentals both stress and tone are present in TNG languages (Foley 2000: 369). Donohue (1997) did a short survey of tone systems in New Guinea. He proposes a classificatory system of pitch accent, word tone and syllable tone. Kewa has both stress and tone (Franklin 1971). Kewapi stress is rule governed. The language has a word tone system with both register and contour tone patterns. It contrasts high tone — *pú* 'go' and low tone *pù* 'urine'. These level tones are realised as high-low and low-high contours on monosyllabic words — *pû* 'relative' high-low (i.e. a falling tone) and *pǔ* 'liver' low-high (i.e. a rising tone) respectively.

Morphological types in the languages of New Guinea differ. They include isolating, agglutinative, synthetic (e.g. many languages of the Trans New Guinea family) and polysynthetic languages (e.g. the Kiwai and Lower Sepik-Ramu language family (Foley 2000: 370). Kewapi is more synthetic but it also possesses slightly polysynthetic features in the sense that a good number of its enclitics realise a fusion of grammatical categories, especially the enclitics *-me*, *-de*, *-da*, *-na*, *-pe* and *-re*. There are both enclitics and affixes. Most affixes are suffixes like many TNG languages (Wurm 1982: 80). The only two prefixes are negative and causative prefixes. The morphology of nouns and verbs are complex, especially of verbs.

Nouns. Kewapi nominal categories that can be marked on the noun are kinship relation, definite/indefinite status, diminution/augmentation, quantity and case. Nouns can be specified for dual, paucal, and plural number, unlike many TNG languages that do not inflect for number (Foley 2000: 371). The overt two-gender systems appearing in pronouns, adjectives and nouns and verb markers found in some TNG languages (Wurm 1982: 80) are absent in Kewapi and generally the Engan family (Franklin 1997: 188). The covert classification of nouns through the use of classificatory verbs in the West-Central TNG languages like Enga (Lang 1973, 1975) is present in Kewa (Franklin 1981). Kewapi uses the verbs *aa* 'stand', *pisa* 'sit' and *sa* 'put' as existential *be* verbs for classifying nouns, e.g. *winya* 'woman', *wena* 'fish', *ipa* 'water', etc. belong to one class in that they take the verb *pisa* 'sit', *repona* 'tree', *remo* 'evil spirit', *mena* 'pig', etc. take *aa* 'stand' and *kaana* 'stone', *su* 'land', *kaare* 'car', etc. take *sa* 'put'. Nominals are case-marked *-me/-*

mi 'ergative' (subject), *-pora* 'locative', *-nane* 'directive', *-na* 'genitive/benefactive' and *-mi* 'instrumental'. Kewapi uses the ergative marker to identify the subject of transitive verbs. The most actor-like role marked by the ergative marker is selected as subject of a transitive verb.

Pronouns. Kewapi has nine free personal pronouns. Each pronoun has singular, dual and plural number. In addition, there are verbal pronominal suffixes which distinguish first, second and third persons. Singular, dual and plural numbers are distinguished for the first and second persons, but the third person *-na/-nya* does not distinguish number. There are distinct suffixes for inclusive and exclusive, perhaps an idiosyncratic feature of Kewa. These pronominal suffixes function as switch-reference markers in coordinate medial clauses that are temporally or aspectually linked to the final clauses.

Verbs. Kewapi has ditransitive, transitive and intransitive verbs. Verbal categories that can be marked on the verb are negation, causation, direction, split-action, aspect, subject-tense, evidence and illocutionary act. The last two categories are marked by enclitics whereas the others are marked by affixes. Like most TNG languages (Foley 2000: 377) Kewapi has subject agreement which is portmanteau with tense inflection in the declarative clause. Kewapi distinguishes morphologically five tenses – future, present, near past, remote past and simple present which covers simple present and habitual tenses. Habitual tense is indicated by durative suffixes or nominalised predicates that take the simple present tense. Subject-tense categories are morphologically distinct from directional and aspectual categorises. The directional category contrasts upward and downward directions. The aspectual category contrasts completive, non-completive, durative and continuative aspects - all are morphologically distinguished. Like many TNG languages (Foley 2000: 381) Kewapi verbs are morphologically marked for irrealis status and has realis verb forms. Verbs are also marked for intentional and desiderative modalities. Two valence increasing derivational processes are causative verb derivation and benefactive verb derivation. Both intransitive and transitive verb bases can be used to derive causative verbs by the derivational prefix *ma-* 'CAUS'. Benefactive verbs are derived from both activity intransitive and transitive verbs. This derivation occurs through a morphophonemic change with alters the word-final vowels /a, i, u, or ə/ to /a:/, a long central vowel, to derive a benefactive verb. The valence of some transitive verbs can be reduced by one argument (subject) by the detransitiving suffix *-ba/-bi*. Incorporation of nouns, adverbials and deictic elements on the verb, commonly found in highly polysynthetic languages like Yimas (Foley 2000: 381), is not found in Kewapi, showing that Kewapi is basically a synthetic language.

Syntax. Syntactically languages fall into left-headed (head + complement) and right-headed (complement + head) (Foley 2000: 382). Kewapi is right-headed with SOV constituent order. In Nichols' (1986) typology of head-marking and dependent-marking morphosyntax, Kewapi has both head-marking and dependent-marking morphosyntax. In a possessive noun phrase, the possessor (dependent) is marked. In a transitive clause the subject nominal (dependent) is marked by the ergative marker and the verb (head) is marked by a subject agreement suffix. Clause chaining (which distinguishes independent and dependent clauses) and switch reference found in TNG languages is present in Kewapi, but the switch-reference morphology is not as complex as those found in the Eastern Highlands languages (Scott 1978), where there are up to three sets of switch-reference subject agreement morphemes. Kewapi coordinate dependent verbs are marked for interclausal reference and temporal and aspectual relation with the independent clauses. The temporal and aspectual suffixes of dependent verbs are distinct from those of independent verbs. The dependent clause is at least dependent on the final clause's mood and tense (for declarative clauses). Negative polarity can be marked independently on dependent clauses. Apart from clause chaining, Kewapi has serial verb constructions (SVCs) and verbal adjuncts. Up to four verbs can occur in a series. Serial verbs are used to express durative aspect (the verb *pisa* 'sit' in the final position expresses durative aspect of the preceding verb), purpose (the preceding transitive verb becomes the purpose for the realisation of the following motion verb), manner (morphological causative verbs express manner of realisation of the preceding verb), etc. Verbal adjuncts consist of noun + generic or light verb, e.g., *kone sa* 'thought put = think'.

Discourse and genre. Discourse cohesion is established through tail-head linkages, the use of deictic elements plus subordinators, e.g., *go pea-daa* 'that do.it-because = because of that' and coordinators, e.g. *go pu-maa* 'that do-SEQ.SS = having done that' and the linker *ade* 'seen' mainly in narratives. In other words, as Foley (2000: 357) states, discourse structures are highly elliptical with the verbal morphology providing signals for the recovery of elided information and the cohesion of the text. Rhetorical questions occur predominately in explanatory or argumentative genres. The verbal structure *li-sa-na* 'say-3SG.RPT-GEN' is extensively used in narrative texts to mark the viewing of an event from the actor's viewpoint. As stated by Foley (2000: 387) for New Guinea languages, information structure notions like topic and focus are superimposed upon the basic clause unit in Kewapi by the use of the enclitics *-re* 'TOPIC' and *-da* 'FOCUS'. As mentioned above, these enclitics realise other semantic categories, e.g. , *-re* marks conditional clauses, topic-as-subject in verb-less constructions, backgrounded or reactivated structures, etc and *-da* marks indefinite nominals, predicate or clausal focus, contrastive focus clause in constructions with negative polarity, etc. Constituent order is used to signal topic (backgrounded nominals) and focus (foregrounded nominals). In the SOV word order, the subject nominal coincides with topic (although subject is a morphosyntactic notion), and object coincides with focus. The subject nominal is under pragmatically marked focus status when it occupies the preverbal slot and the object nominal is topicalised by occupying the topic slot.

3. Coordinate structures of Kewapi

Section 3.1 looks at coordinate independent constructions and section 3.2 deals with constructions with coordinate dependent clauses.

The definition of a coordinate clause adopted in the following description is from Foley (1986: 177). A coordinate clause is one which does not function as an argument of the main clause and is not an embedded part within a whole, but is one which is in a coordinate relation with the initial or final clause.

Foley (1986) draws a distinction for Papuan languages between coordinate independent - those sentences in which each independent clause selects core and peripheral arguments, tense and mood - and coordinate dependent (or co-subordinate) constructions, which depend for some or all of these elements on their specification in another clause, usually the sentence-final clause.

Kewapi has two categories of coordinate sentences: (1) a sentence consisting of coordinate independent clauses and (2) a sentence consisting of a coordinate dependent and a coordinate independent clauses. The latter type has two conjoined subtypes (1) coordinate dependent clauses with no verbal suffixes and (2) coordinate dependent clauses marked by interclausal reference suffixes.

The following examples contrast the various coordinate constructions. (1), a coordinate independent construction, contrasts with (2-4), coordinate dependent constructions.

In a sentence with two coordinate independent clauses, both the initial and the final clauses select core and peripheral arguments, tense and mood independently. In (1), the initial coordinate independent clause has the intransitive verb *epa* 'come', which is suffixed by a third person singular subject agreement and near present tense suffix *-a* and is followed by the coordinate linker *pere* 'but'. The final coordinate independent clause of sentence (1) has another intransitive verb *aa* 'stand/stay' and is suffixed by a third person singular and near present tense suffix *-ripa*. The subject referents of the initial and the final independent clauses are different persons. The initial and the final clauses also select their own peripheral NPs (*ada* 'house' and *Mendi* respectively). Although both the initial and final coordinate independent clauses in this example select the same tense (near past tense) and mood (declarative), these categories may be different in other sentences with coordinate independent clauses.

(1) *Ali   ada   epa-a   pere,*
    man   house   come-3SG.NPT   but,
    were   Mendi   pa   aa-ripa.
    wife   Mendi   just   stay-3SG.NPT
    'The man came home, but his wife just stayed at Mendi.'

(2) is a sentence consisting of a sequence of coordinate dependent clauses and a coordinate independent clause. The sequence of coordinate dependent clauses *ali-mi ada elo*, *maapu su* and *winya lamu* depends on the final finite clause for subject, tense and mood, but each clause selects its own object nominal *ada* 'house', *maapu* 'garden' or *winya* 'woman'. The scope of the verb *pi* 'do' includes all the verbs, i.e., it is the main verb on which the rest depend.

(2) *Ali-mi   ada   elo*
    man-ERG   house   build
    maapu   su
    garden   put
    winya   lamu   pi-sa.
    woman   marry   do-3SG.RPT
    'The man built a house, made a garden, and married a wife.'

(3) is a sentence with a coordinate dependent clause marked by a temporal and same subject (SS) suffix and a coordinate independent clause. The coordinate dependent clause is marked by a simultaneous SS suffix -*ri*, which indicates that the actions of the initial and the final clauses are realised simultaneously by the same actor (or subject). In a sentence with a coordinate dependent clause the temporal suffix that indicates temporal relation of the dependent and final clauses also signals same subject (SS) relation with the final clause (see Franklin 1971, 1983 and Yarapea 2001).

(3) *Nogo   agaale   la-ri,   epi-sa.*
    girl   talk   say-SIM.SS   come-3SG.RPT
    'As the girl was talking, she came.'

(4) is a sentence with a coordinate dependent clause which is marked by a switch-reference marker and a temporal suffix. It contrasts with (2) and (3) because it has switch reference. The coordinate dependent clause selects its own subject, but it is dependent on the final clause for tense and mood. The suffix -lomaa 'SEQ' links the coordinate dependent and the coordinate final clauses. In such a construction the subject suffix of the coordinate dependent clause signals that the subject of the following or sentence-final clause is different from the subject of the coordinate dependent clause (see 3.2.2.2 below).

(4)   *Winya   pe-na-lomaa,   nogo epi-sa.*
       woman   go-3SG.DS-SEQ,   girl   come-3SG.RPT
       'The woman had gone, and then the girl came.' Or 'After the woman had gone, the girl came.'

In the following sections each of the above coordinate construction types introduced in 3.0 will be described in some detail. Section 3.1 will illustrate and discuss sentences with coordinate independent clauses and section 3.2 will describe coordinate dependent construction types.

3.1 Coordinate independent constructions

As illustrated in (1), Kewapi has coordinate sentences with coordinate independent clauses. Such clauses are limited to those linked by the conjunctions *pere* 'but' and *-pa* 'or'. These conjunctions form a unit with the preceding clause, not the following clause. It appears to be a general characteristic of verb-final languages that an interclausal conjunction forms a unit with the previous clause, whereas it forms a unit with the following clause in verb-medial languages like English (see Longacre 1985: 239, Payne 1997: 338).

3.1.1 *pere* 'but'

As in (8.1), *pere* 'but' functions as a coordinator, which denotes contrast between propositions. It signals that the marked clause is in a coordinate relation with the following clause, as exemplified in (1). The coordinator may also be used as a discourse linker, as in (5).

(5) Go   li-sa   pere,
    that   say-3SG.RPT   but,
    Kiwai-mi to-a-me   ya-daa
    Kiwai-ERG say-3SG.FUT-INST   be-RSN
    dia   li-sa.
    no   say-3SG.RPT
    'She said that, but Kiwai said no.'

In (5) *go* 'that' refers back to an ellipsed clause. It substitutes the elided clause and functions as an object argument of the initial coordinate verb. The coordinator *pere* 'but' links the initial coordinate clause to the following clause. In the context of (5) the ellipsed clause presents the proposition that Kiwai and Suli cannot get married because they are related (Thesis), but Kiwai said no, i.e., Kiwai said that he will marry Suli despite the fact that they are relatives (Anithesis). Franklin (1971: 115) calls such sentences "Antithetical sentences".

3.1.2 *-pa* 'or'

A sentence whose initial clause is marked by *-pa* 'or' is semantically an alternative coordinate construction because both clauses in such a construction express alternative events. The mood of such a construction is interrogative, which is signalled either formally by an interrogative marker *-ya* or prosodically by a rising question intonation. Consider the following hypothetical examples.

In sentence (6a) the speaker is seeking either a 'yes' or a 'no' answer. The interrogative mood of the sentence is marked formally by the interrogative mood marker -*ya*.

(6a) *Ne   pa-li-pa*
      you   go-2SG.FUT-or
      na-pa-li-ya?
      NEG-go-2SG.FUT-Q
      'Will you go or will you not go?'

It is possible to abbreviate or shorten sentence (6a) by only uttering the first clause, as in (6b). The ellipsed negative alternative clause is replaced by the copula verb *ya* 'be', to which is attached the alternative clause marker -*pa*. The negative meaning is understood in the context of the construction because the expected answer to the question in (6b) is either a 'yes' or a 'no'.

(6b) *Ne   pa-li   ya-pa?*
      you   go-2SG.FUT   be-or?
      'Will you go or not?'

In predicate nominal constructions the alternative marker -*pa* (or its variants -*paa* or -*pae*) is attached to the verb *ya* 'be', as in (7a-c). These constructions are structurally similar, but semantically dissimilar. Note that in (7a) the mood of the sentence is signalled formally, whereas in (7b-c), it is expressed by a question intonation. By asking the question (7a), the speaker is seeking confirmation that what the speaker is seeing at a distance is indeed a pig.

(7a) *Mogo-re,   mena   ya-paa*
      that-TOP,   pig   be-or
      álí-ya?
      what-Q
      'As for that, is it a pig or what?'

When the form *yapa(a)* is recursive in a predicate nominal construction, as in (7b), or any other construction, this tends to signal that the speaker does not have any preconception about the validity of the range of alternative possibilities.

(7b)   *Mogo-re,*   *mena*   *ya-paa*
         that-TOP,   pig   be-or
         álí   *ya-pa?*
         what   be-or
         'As for that, is it a pig or what is it?'

The speaker normally requires an answer for an alternative question like (7b), whereas an answer is not normally required for a construction like (7c). In (7c) the speaker is really expressing uncertainty, i.e., he is not certain about the possible events of the predicates. This meaning is formally signalled by *-pae*. Note that the vowels *ae* in *-pae* is the diphthong /æ/.

(7c)   *Mogo-re,*   *mena*   *ya-paa*
         that-TOP,   pig   be-or
         álí   *ya-pae?*
         what   be-or
         'As for that, is it a pig or what can it be?'

Sentence (8) is another construction with the first alternative clause marked by -paa and the final clause marked by -pae to express the speaker's uncertainty.

(8)   *Roto-me*   *ta-a-paa*
        stick-INST   hit-3SG.NPT-or
        álí-mí   *ta-a-pae?*
        what-INST   hit-3SG.NPT-or
        'Did s/he hit someone/thing with a stick or what did s/he hit her/him/it with?'

The predicate *yapa* can be used recursively to link a number of clauses when the speaker presents several possible events, as (9) shows.

(9) ..*abi-ri   álí   maa   epa-no   ya-pa?,*
    now-TOP what   take   come-1SG be-or,
    nogo-naaki kupi   riaa   epa-no   ya-pa?,
    girl-boy   hug   carry come-1SG be-or,
    sapi-waali   maa   epa-no   ya-pa?
    sweet potato-sugar cane take come-1SG be-or
    lo,   go   rupa   ta   epa-wa-de.
    say,   that like   say   come-1SG.NPT-DEF
    '..now, what should I bring or, should I bring children or, should I bring food or?,' I came to speak thus.

In (9) *yapa* is used three times following the sequence of coordinate dependent clauses expressing alternative possibilities. These clauses occur as object complement clauses of the verb *lo* 'say'. The clause following the complement-taking verb occurs as a rephrased clause where *go* 'that' refers back to the preceding clause whose matrix verb is *lo* 'say'.

3.2 Coordinate dependent constructions

As introduced in section 3.0, a coordinate dependent construction clause has two subtypes (1) conjoined coordinate dependent clauses with no verbal suffixes and (2) a coordinate dependent clause marked according to whether its subject is the same as or different from the subject of the following clause. Each of these subtypes will be discussed in some detail in the following sections, but first the distinctive features of coordinate dependent verbs in Kewapi are outlined.

Verbs of coordinate dependent clauses have been referred to as medial verbs in Kewa (see Franklin 1971, 1983) because they not only occur sentence-medially or non-finally, but importantly because they share certain grammatical categories of the sentence-final clauses. A coordinate medial verb in Kewapi can be characterised as one that:

(1) lacks tense marking;
(2) shares the mood (and tense in declarative clauses) of the following or sentence-final clause; and/or,
(3) is marked according to whether its subject is the same as or is different from the subject of the following clause.

In the following discussion of coordinate constructions, the mention of a coordinate dependent clause will assume the presence of its coordinate independent clause counterpart to reduce repetitive mention of this pairing. On occasions the use of the phrases 'medial clauses or verbs' and 'final (finite) clauses or verbs' will refer to the same members of the pairing of a coordinate dependent clause and a coordinate independent clause.

3.2.1   Conjoined coordinate dependent clauses

Conjoined coordinate dependent clauses share subject, tense and mood categories with those of the following or final clauses. Furthermore, the final verb of conjoined dependent clauses that are not marked by verbal suffixes is always the verb *pea* 'to do', as in (10), previously given as (2).

In (10) the sequence of medial verbs depends on the final clause for subject, tense and mood. The actions of the medial verbs are realised by the same actor but the medial verbs have their own object nominals *ada* 'house', *maapu* 'garden' and *winya* 'woman' respectively.

(10) *Ali-mi   ada   elo*
       man-ERG   house   build
       maapu   su
       garden   put
       winya   lamu   pi-sa.
       woman   marry   do-3SG.RPT
       'The man built a house, made a garden, and married a wife.'

A series of 'coordinated' activities done by different actors may be expressed by medial clauses, as in (11). In (11) there are three medial clauses preceding the final finite clause. These medial verbs are not marked for subject, tense and mood and so are dependent on these categories on the final clause. All the medial verbs have different subject and object nominals. The subject nominals of the medial verbs are cross-referenced in the final verb by the third person plural subject agreement suffix *-simi*. (11) is not a switch-reference marking construction. The medial clauses are conjoined (but not embedded) under the main verb *pi* 'do' as indicated by the subject-tense suffix *-simi* '3PL.RPT'.

(11) *Nogo-me   kaai   ware*
      girl-ERG   banana   peel
      naaki-mi   repona   rele-pu
      boy-ERG   wood   split-do
      winya-me   repona   kiru
      woman-ERG   wood   burn
      ali-mi   mena   lu   pi-simi.
      man-ERG   pig   hit   do-3PL.RPT

'The girl peeled bananas, the boy split wood, the woman burned the wood, and the man slaughtered a pig.'

3.2.2 'Switch-reference' constructions

A coordinate dependent clause is marked to indicate whether the subject referent of the following or sentence-final coordinate clause is the same (SS) or is different subject (DS) referent. In other words, a coordinate dependent clause is marked for "interclausal" reference (Franklin 1983). The term switch-reference will be reserved for DS constructions.

Section 3.2.2.1 and 3.2.2.2 will describe respectively SS and DS constructions.

3.2.2.1 'Same-subject' constructions

A coordinate dependent clause can be marked for either a simultaneous or a sequential temporal relation with the final clause. A 'simultaneous' temporal relation means that the period of duration of the two actions must overlap, either partially or fully (see Foley 1986: 180). Sequential actions are those in which there is no temporal overlap. The temporal suffixes also signal same subject (SS) reference with the following or sentence-final clause so they are referred to as 'temporal SS' suffixes. Table 1 presents temporal SS suffixes of Kewapi.

Table 1 Kewapi temporal SS suffixes

Suffix	Temporal relation	Verbal context
-ri	simultaneous	transitive
-ra	simultaneous	intransitive
-maa	sequential	intransitive/transitive
-loma	sequential	with intentional mode

The simultaneous SS and the sequential SS suffixes each attach to a medial verb that is not marked for subject.

3.2.2.1.1 Simultaneous suffixes

The simultaneous temporal SS suffixes -ri and -ra suffix coordinate dependent verbs. The former is suffixed to transitive verbs and the latter is suffixed to the intransitive verb *aa* 'stand' in an aspectual verb phrase, as exemplified in the following.

In (12) the actions of the verb-verb adjunct *pake na* 'steal eat = steal' and *pamu* 'go around/travel' are simultaneously accomplished by the same actor, as signalled by *-ri* 'SIM.SS'.

(12) Go   naaki-mi   pake   na-ri,
     that   boy-ERG   steal   eat-SIM.SS
     pamu-la.
     go around-3SG.PRG
     'That boy is stealing, as he is going around.'

While *-ri* 'SIM.SS' suffixes a coordinate medial transitive verb, as in (12 above), *-ra* 'SIM.SS' suffixes the coordinate medial intransitive verb *aa* 'stand', as in (13a-c).

In (13a) the coordinate medial predicate *epa aa-ra* 'come stand-SIM.SS' is a serial predicate in which each verb retains its lexical meaning. The simultaneous and same subject suffix *-ra* links the coordinate medial predicate to the final clause.

(13a) Gu   pu-maa   li-sa-na
      that   do-SEQ.SS   say-3SG.RPT-GEN
      meda-lena   epaa   aa-ra
      one.INDF-LOC   come   stand-SIM.SS
      ta-lo   paki   ya   li-sa.
      say-IRR   half   call   say-3SG.RPT.
      'Having done that, as he came and stood at a place, he would call, "half".'

In (13b) the coordinate medial predicate is a serial predicate *maa tya-lo aa-ra* 'get hit-CONT stand-SIM.SS'. The first member *maa* 'get' functions to indicate change of location of the object nominal (a pig) and the second member *tya-lo* that is marked for continuative aspect provides the lexical content and the last member *aa* 'stand' functions as an auxiliary verb for marking simultaneous and subject relation with the final verb.

(13b) Ne-na   ama-na   mena   laapo
      you-GEN   mother-GEN   pig   two
      maa   tya-lo   aa-ra
      take   hit-CONT   stand-SIM.SS

"*imi*	*pu-lupa!*"	*lo-maa*
you plural	go-2PL"	say-SEQ.SS
lu	*rali-sa-ya..*	
hit	chase-3SG.RPT-NSN..	

'As (he) was slaughtering your mother's two pigs, (he) said, "you plural go away", and he chased you plural away...'

In (13c) the coordinate medial predicate is an aspectual verb phrase formed by a serial predicate *pu-lu aa-ra* 'go-CONT stand-SIM.SS'. Again the last member is suffixed by *-ra* 'SIM.SS' to indicate the simultaneous and same subject relation with the final clause.

(13c)	*Ipu*	*ada*	*pu-lu*	*aa-ra,*
	he	house	go-CONT	stand-SIM.SS,
	ni	*rai-de*	*gi-sa.*	
	I	axe-DEF	give-3SG.RPT	

'As he was going to the house, he gave me the axe.'

3.2.2.1.2 Sequential suffixes

The two sequential SS suffixes *-maa* and *-loma* are in complementary distribution. The latter is obligatorily followed by the instrument marker to indicate intentional action, i.e., semantically the action of the marked clause is intentionally done in order to realise the action of the following clause (as in (15a-b)) and the former occurs elsewhere, as in (14)).

In (14) *no-ma pu-maa-re* 'eat-CONT do-SEQ.SS-TOP' is an aspectual VP where *no* 'eat' is the lexical verb and *pu* 'do' is the auxiliary verb marked by the sequential SS suffix and the topic marker. The action of the VP and the state expressed by *le* 'say/be' occur in a sequence and involve the same subject referent (a piglet). Note that *-ma* in *no-ma* 'eat-CONT' signals continuative aspect rather than sequential relation with the following verb *pu* 'do'.

(14) Go   robo-re,   adu   no-ma   pu-maa-re,
     that   time-TOP,   milk   eat-CONT   do-SEQ.SS-TOP,
     oge-si   adaa   le-a.
     small-DIM   big   say-3SG.SPR
     'At that time it continues to feed on (its mother's) milk and it becomes a bit bigger.'

As in (15a-b), *-loma* and its infrequent variant *-toma* suffix medial verbs that are not marked for subject. The medial verbs share the subject and tense of the immediately following finite clauses, which in both cases is *li-sa-na*. The subject suffix refers to the actor in the narrative that the narrator is narrating. The subject referent of the finite clause in (15a) is the woman character and in (15b) it is the evil man. In the context of (15a) the woman character in the legend intentionally picks up the other half of the evil man that is guarding her, when he does something. The intentional action sense of the medial verb marked by *-toma* 'SEQ.SS' is much clearer in sentence (15b). Here, the evil man (the villain) combines its two halves in order to kill and eat the woman and her husband (the victims).

(15a) Ade   maa   mata-loma-me   li-sa-na,
      DEF   take   carry-SEQ.SS-INST   say-3SG.RPT-GEN,
      o-de   ipu-de   paki   lu
      here-DEF   he-DEF   half   hit
      wi-sa-de-ai   pa   wi-nya   na-pe
      put-3SG.RPT-DEF-NOM   just   leave-3SG   NEG-go
      li-sa-na,   maa   madi-sa..
      say-3SG.RPT-GEN,   take   carry-3SG.RPT
      'After carrying the pork, the other half of himself that the evil man had left behind to guard the woman, was not left behind, she took it and carried it....'

(15b) *Ade   kirita-toma-me*
DEF   combine-SEQ.SS-INST
li-sa-na-re,
say-3SG.RPT-GEN-TOP,
ade   winya   ali-lopo-re
the   woman   man-DL-TOP
go   lu   ni-sa-na-da.
there   hit   eat-3SG.RPT-GEN-INDF

'After combining the two halves, the evil man killed and ate the woman and man.'

3.2.2.2 'Different-subject' constructions

There is no dedicated different subject (DS) suffix (or a set of suffixes) in Kewapi. However, there is a morphologically complex set of markers that always signals DS in certain syntactic contexts, but these apparent DS subject markers also occur in other contexts where they do not signal DS. This complexity is resolved by the following explanations.

(1) It is the combination of the DS suffix plus a temporal or an aspectual marker (including an aspectual verb) that signals switch reference in a coordinate construction.

(2) In contexts where there are no temporal or aspectual markers present, the 'DS' suffixes do not signal switch reference. In such contexts deontic mood is marked or implied.

The set of 'DS' suffixes is presented in Table 2 below.

Table 2 'Different-subject' suffixes of Kewapi

Number	1st Person	2nd Person	3rd Person
Singular	*-no*	*-inya*	*-na* or *-nya*
Dual	*-pono* (excl.)	*-lipinya*	*-na* or *-nya*
Plural	*-mono* (excl.)	*-liminya*	*-na* or *-nya*
	Inclusive Dual: *-pona* '1SG/2SG' Plural: *-minya* '1/2PL'		

The first and second person have singular, dual and plural numbers. The first person has dual and plural exclusive and inclusive suffixes. The third person does not code number.

Table 3 presents temporal and aspectual suffixes which obligatorily mark the DS marked coordinate-dependent verbs to signal switch reference.

Table 3 Kewapi temporal and aspectual suffixes

Temporal suffix	Aspectual suffixes	Verbal contexts
-lomaa 'sequential'	*-lo* 'continuative'	Transitive verb + *-lo* + *aa* 'stand' or *pisa* 'sit'
	-lu 'continuative'	Intransitive verb + *-lu* + *aa* 'stand' or *pisa* 'sit'

The choice of the posture verbs *aa* 'stand' and *pisa* 'sit' depends on the speaker's perception of the actor's posture in realising the event of the aspectual verb phrase in which the continuative aspectual suffixes: *-lo* and *-lu* occur. While this observation holds in most cases, it is also possible for activities done standing to occur with *pisa* 'sit', e.g. *no pu-lu pisa-no gae te-a* 'down there go-CONT sit-1SG. DS dark say/be-3SG.FUT = As I am going down there, it will get dark.' In cases like this, the activity is perceived to be done at a slow pace.

As stated above, a switch-reference construction is one in which the coordinate dependent verb is suffixed by both a DS subject suffix and a temporal or an aspectual suffix. A temporal or an aspectual suffix is necessary to link the coordinate dependent clause to the following or sentence-final coordinate independent clause. Consider the following constructions showing temporal and aspectual marking of the switch-reference marking clauses.

The only temporal suffix that may be suffixed to the switch-reference marking clause is *-lomaa* 'SEQ', seen in (16a-b) is distinct from the sequential SS suffixes *-maa* and *-loma* in Table 1 above. In (16b), the DS suffix *-nya*, whose referent is the one half of the evil man that guards the woman, signals that the subject referent of the immediate verb *li* 'say' is different. The subject referent of *li* 'say' is the other half of the evil man that goes away hastily.

(16a) *Winya   pe-na-lomaa,   nogo   ipi-sa.*
      woman   go-3SG.DS-SEQ,   girl   come-3SG.RPT
      'The woman had gone, and the girl came.'

(16b) *..mo-de   winya   pa*
      ..FHL-DEF   woman   just

      surubu   pa   piri-nya-lomaa
      guard   just   sit-3SG.DS-SEQ

      ipu-de   mo   medane   li-sa-na,
      he-DEF   FHL   one half   say-3SG.RPT-GEN,

      ipu   maa   pili   tya-ba   pa-sa..
      he   take   shoot   hit-PUNCT   go-3SG.RPT..

      '..one half stayed to guard the woman and the other half went down hastily (to go as an arrow that had been shot)...'

A coordinate-dependent serial predicate is suffixed by a DS suffix to signal switch reference, as in (17a-b).

In (17a) the coordinate-dependent serial predicate consists of *po rele pea-lo aa-liminya* 'chop split do-CONT stand-2PL.DS = while you plural were chopping and splitting the tree'. The first verb *po* 'chop' and the second verb *rele* 'split' provide the lexical meanings. The third verb *pea* 'do' functions as an auxiliary verb expressing continuative aspect and the final verb *aa* 'stand' also functions as an auxiliary verb for marking the DS suffix *-liminya* '2PL.DS', which signals that the subject referent of the final clause is different, i.e., *-wa* '1SG'.

(17a) *Ni-ri,   po   rele   pea-lo   aa-liminya,*
      I-TOP,   chop   split   do-CONT   stand-2PL.DS,
      epa-wa-de.
      come-1SG.NPT-DEF
      'As for me, I came while you were chopping and splitting the tree.'

In (17b) the coordinate-dependent serial predicate consists of *pu-lu piri-nya* 'go-CONT sit-3SG.DS'. The lexical content comes from *pu* 'go' and *piri* 'sit' is in auxiliary function so it is suffixed by the DS suffix *-nya* '3SG.DS'.

(17b) *Ipu   ada   pu-lu   piri-nya   ádá-pe.*
      he   house   go-CONT   sit-3SG.DS   see-2DL.NPT
      'As he was going home, you two saw him.'

In the presence of the temporal sequence suffix *-lomaa* and an aspectually marked serial predicate a DS suffix signals that the subject referent of the following or sentence-final clause must be a different subject referent from itself. The DS suffix does not specify the person and number of the following subject referent which it signals. All it does is simply signal that the following subject is to be considered a different referent from itself.

Another type of switch reference construction is one in which the coordinate dependent verb is a stative verb and is marked by a DS suffix in a coordinate construction. Consider (18a-c).

(18a) *Ne   aa-inya   ni   epa-wa.*
      you   stand-2SG.DS   I   come-1SG.NPT
      'As you were standing, I came.'

(18b) *Ni   pisa-no   ipu   eda   ni-sa*
      I   sit-1SG.DS   he   food   eat-3SG.RPT
      'While I was sitting, he ate food.'
(18c) *Wi-nya   pu.*
      leave-3SG.DS   go
      'Leave it and go.'

In (18a-c) the coordinate dependent verbs are all stative: *aa* 'stand' in (18a), *pisa* 'sit' in (18b) and *wi* 'leave' in (18c). These stative verbs retain their lexical meanings and also code durative aspectual meanings, i.e., they are aspectual verbs. When they are marked by the DS suffixes they signal switch reference. The difference between these stative verbs and the aspectually marked serial predicates is that in a serial verb lexical meaning is expressed by one or two members, aspectual meaning is marked on another member and the switch reference is marked on the last member of the serial predicate, as in (17a-b) above.

3.2.2.2.1 Non-switch reference constructions

There are various circumstances in which a 'DS' subject suffix occurs alone, i.e., without a tense or aspectual suffix/verb, and in such contexts there is no obvious syntactic reason to believe that the marked clauses occur as switch-reference signalling clauses. These circumstances are:
a) appositional and alternative constructions;
b) embedded constructions; and,
c) independent clause constructions.
It is the case that (a), (b) and (c) form a semantic set: they all entail deontic modality, except in (b) where desiderative modality is expressed when the 'DS' marked clause is the complement clause of the verb *yaa* 'want' (see (20c) and (21) below).

The 'DS' marked clause occurs as an independent clause. Such a clause is a subjunctive mood clause, so the 'DS' marked clause will henceforth be referred to as a subjunctive clause in contexts where switch reference is not signalled by the 'DS' suffix to differentiate DS constructions from non-switch-reference constructions.

3.2.2.2.1.1 Juxtaposed constructions

In circumstances where two or more clauses are in juxtaposition or alternation, the subjunctive clause marked by the 'DS' suffix but not by a temporal or aspectual suffix or verb does not signal switch reference, but expresses deontic modality, as (19a-c) show.

In (19a) there are two subjunctive clauses in juxtaposition and both encode deontic modality. The 'DS' suffix in each clause does not signal switch reference.

(19a) Ne   sapi   na-inya   gia-no.
       you   sweet potato   eat-2SG   give-1SG
       'You should eat sweet potato (so) I should give it to you.'

In (19b) the initial subjunctive clause is in apposition with the final imperative clause. The 'DS' suffix of the initial clause does not signal switch reference but expresses deontic modal meaning.

(19b) Ne   sapi   na-inya pu.
       you   sweet potato   eat-2SG go
       'You should eat sweet potato (so) go.'

In (19c) the three subjunctive clauses (shown in bold face), which occur as alternative clauses, all express deontic modality.

(19c) ..abi-ri   **áli**   maa   epa-no   ya-pa?,
       now-TOP   what   take   come-1SG.   be-or,
       nogo-naaki   kupi   riaa   epa-no   ya-pa?,
       girl-boy   hug   carry   come-1SG   be-or,
       sapi-waali   maa   epa-no   ya-pa?
       kaukau-sugar cane   take   come-1SG   be-or

lo	*go*	*rupa*	*ta*	*epa-wa-de.*
say	that	like	say	come-1SG.NPT-DEF

..now, what should I bring or, should I bring children or, should I bring food or?", I came to say like that.'

3.2.2.2.1.2 Embedded constructions

In embedded constructions, the subjunctive clause marked by the 'DS' suffix also expresses deontic modality, except with the complement-taking verb (CTV) *yaa* 'want', where desiderative modality is expressed. The common embedded construction types are complement clauses of the four main CTVs *la* 'say' (as in (20a)), *kone sa* 'think' (as in (20b)), *yaa* 'want' (as in (20c)), and *paga* 'listen' (as in (20d)).

(20a) *Né-mé   [ni   po-no]   la-wa-de.*
      I-ERG [I   go-1SG]   say-1SG.NPT-DEF
      'I said ,"I should go".'

(20b) *Né-mé   [ne   pa-inya]*
      I-ERG [you   go-2SG]
      kone   sa-wa-de.
      thought   put-1SG.NPT-DEF
      'I thought, "you should go".'

(20c) ***Bob-me   [**Mary pe-nya]*
      Bob-ERG   [Mary go-3SG]
      yaa   pi-a
      want   do-3SG.SPR
      'Bob wants Mary to leave.'

(20d) *[...agi   araa-lopo-me   ta-pe   pi]*
      [mother   father-DL-ERG   say-IRR what]
      paga-pona...
      listen-1DL
      'We should listen to what the parents are going to say.'

As in (20d), the CTV *paga* 'listen' occurs with the complementiser *pi* 'what'. Note that, as in (20c), when the desiderative verb *yaa* 'want' takes a subjunctive clause as its complement clause, the deontic sense of the subjunctive clause is suppressed by the desiderative meaning.

The CTV *yaa* 'want' that takes a subjunctive clause as its complement clause may be marked by the causal subordinator *-daa* 'because' to form a subordinate clause, as in (21).

(21) Ne   pa-inya   ya-daa   la-lo.
     you   go-2SG   want-because   say-1SG.PRG
     'Because I want you to go, I am saying it.'

Only the subordinator *-le* 'because' may mark a subjunctive clause to form a subordinate clause and the matrix clause may be either an imperative clause (as in (22a)), or a subjunctive clause (as in (22b)), but not a declarative or an interrogative clause.

(22a) Ne   pa-inya-le   ipu.
      you   go-2SG-because   come
      'Because you should go, come.'

(22b) Ne   pa-inya-le   rai   mea-inya.
      you   go-2SG-because   axe   get-2SG
      'Because you must go, you should get the axe.'

In (22a-b) the subordinate subjunctive clauses retain their deontic meanings.

3.2.2.2.1.3 Independent constructions

As in appositional, alternative and embedded constructions, the subjunctive clause as an independent clause expresses deontic modality, as in (23a), or in (23b), where the subjunctive clause is a matrix clause.

(23a) *Ne   pa-inya.*
      you   go-1SG
      'You should go.'

(23b) *Abi-ri   tukiloko pea-a-na-le*
      now-TOP   two o'clock do-3SG.NPT-GEN-because
      po-no.
      go-1SG
      'Because it is two o'clock, I should go.'

To conclude, subjunctive clauses that are marked by distinctive subject suffixes hitherto referred to as 'DS' suffixes only signal switch reference when the clauses are also marked by either temporal or aspectual markers (including aspectual verbs) in coordinate constructions. In most other constructions such as appositional, alternative, and embedded constructions, the subjunctive clause expresses deontic modality, which is the meaning that is expressed when a subjunctive clause occurs as an independent clause. Thus the present account of switch reference in Kewapi differs from Franklin's (1971, 1983) account of switch reference in Kewa or West Kewa. In Franklin's accounts the 'DS' suffixes signal switch reference, whether explicitly or implicitly, in all syntactic contexts. This is clearly not the case, at least in Kewapi.

Abbreviations

1	first person
2	second person
3	third person
ASP	aspect
AUG	augmentative mode
AVP	auxiliary verb phrase
Ben	beneficiary
CAUS	causative
CDL	close downward location
CHL	close horizontal location
COMPL	completive aspect
CONT	continuative aspect
CTV	complement-taking verb
CUL	close upward location
DEF	definite referent
DES	desiderative modality
DHL	distant horizontal location
DIR	directional marker
DL	dual number
DOWN	downward direction
DS	different subject or switch reference
DUR	durative aspect
ERG	ergative marker
EXCL	exclusive
FDL	far downward location
FHL	far horizontal location
FUL	far upward location
FUT	future tense
GEN	genitive marker
IMM	immediate command
IMP	imperative
INCEP	inceptive aspect
incl.	inclusive
INDF	indefinite referent
INST	instrumental case

intr	intransitive verb
IRR	irrealis status
KIN	kinship marker
lit	literal meaning
LOC	locative marker
MDL	mid downward location
MHL	mid horizontal location
MUL	mid upward location
N	noun
NDL	near downward location
NEG	negative
NHL	near horizontal location
NOM	nominaliser
NON-IMM	non-immediate command
NON-SING	non-singular number
NP	noun phrase
NPT	near past tense
NSN	not seen evidence/event
NUL	near upward location
O	object of transitive verb
Pat	patient
PAUC	paucal number
PERF	perfect aspect
PL	plural
POS	possessor
POSS	possessed
PRG	present progressive tense
PT	participial verb
PUNCT	punctual aspect
PUR	purpose
Q	question
RHL	remote horizontal location
RPT	remote past tense
RQ	rhetoric question
RSN	reason
S	subject of intransitive verb

sec.	section
SEQ	sequence
SG	singular
SIM	simultaneous
SOV	subject-verb-object
SPN	split-action
SPR	simple present tense
SR	switch-reference
SS	same subject
SUB	subject
SUBJ	subjunctive
SV	subject-verb
TNS	tense
TOP	topic
tr	transitive verb
UP	upward direction
V	verb
VP	verb phrase

Note

1. Kewapi is the name given by the speakers of the east dialect of the language described in Franklin (1971 and elsewhere) as 'Kewa'. The author, a native speaker of Kewapi, earned a PhD from the ANU for his thesis 'Morphosyntax of Kewapi' in 2006.

References

Donohue, M. 1997. Tone systems in New Guinea. *Linguistic Typology* 1: 347-386.

Farr, C. J. M. 1999. *The interface between syntax and discourse in Korafe, a Papuan language of Papua New Guinea*. Canberra: Pacific Linguistics, C-148.

Foley, W.A. 1986. *The Papuan languages of New Guinea*. Cambridge: Cambridge.

Foley, W.A. 2000. The Languages of New Guinea. *Ann. Rev. Anthropol.* 29: 357-404.

Franklin, K. J. 1981. Existential and pro-verbs in Kewa. In K. J. Franklin (ed.) *Syntax and semantics in Papua New Guinea languages*, 151-172. Ukarumpa: Summer Institute of Linguistics, Papua New Guinea Branch.

Franklin, K. J. 1983. Some features of interclausal reference in Kewa. In J. Haiman and P. Munro (eds) *Switch reference and universal grammar*, 39-49. Amsterdam/Philadelphia: John Benjamins.

Franklin, K. J. 1997. Engan pronouns and their old endings. *Australian Journal of Linguistics*. 17: 185-217.

Franklin, K. J. 2001. Kutubuan (Foe and Fasu) and Proto Engan. In A. Pawley., M. Ross and D. Tryon (eds) *The boy from Bundaberg: Studies in Melanesian linguistics in honour of Tom Dutton*, 143-154. Pacific Linguistics.

Franklin, K.J. 1971. *A grammar of Kewa, New Guinea*. Canberra: Pacific Linguistics, C16.

James, D. 1983. Verb serialization in Siane. *Journal of Language and Linguistics in Melanesia*, 14 (1/2): 26-75.

Lang, A. 1973. *Enga dictionary*. Canberra: Pacific Linguistics. C-20.

Lang, A. 1975. *The semantics of classificatory verbs in Enga (and other Papua New Guinea languages)*. Pacific Linguistics. B39.

Longacre, R. 1985. Sentences as combination of clauses. In Shopen (ed.) 1985: 235-286.

Nichols, J. 1986. Head-marking and dependent-marking grammar. *Language*, 62(4):56-119.

Payne, T. 1997. *Describing morphosyntax: A guide for field linguists*. Cambridge: Cambridge University Press.

Roberts, J. R. 1997. Switch-Reference in Papua New Guinea. In A. Pawley (ed.) *Papers in Papuan Linguistics* No. 3, 101-241. Canberra: Pacific Linguistics A-87.

Scott, G. 1978. *The Fore language of Papua New Guinea*. Pacific Linguistics. B74.

Wurm, S. 1975. Eastern Central Trans-New Guinea Phylum languages. In S. Wurm(ed.) *New*

Guinea area languages and language study, vol. 1: Papuan languages and the New Guinea linguistic scene, 461-526. Pacific Linguistics C38.

Wurm, S. A. 1982. *The Papuan Languages of Oceania*. Tübingen, Germany: Narr

Yarapea, A.M. 2001. On interclausal reference in Kewa. In A. Pawley, M. Ross and D. Tyron (eds) *The boy from Bundaberg: Studies in Melanesian linguistics in honour of Tom Dutton*, 399-417. Canberra: Pacific Linguistics.

Preservation of Endangered Languages: Issues and Problems

Ruth Saovana-Spriggs
Australian National University

1. Introduction

Local languages in whatever state they are; whether they are in danger of decline or complete extinction or whether they are healthy, all ought to be given the same treatment in language preservation activities. Any local vernacular could show signs of good health when in actual fact, much decline might have occurred, particularly in the cultural content.

Vernacular literacy aimed at early childhood education as a form of language and cultural preservation is a good start but is not substantial. It does not capture nor contain a vast and difficult cultural and linguistics body of material. There is therefore the need to do much more in-depth work in the area than what is currently being done and is available in early vernacular literacy programmes.

Third World countries need to be assisted in rather vigorous and interesting ways of documenting and preserving their local languages and cultures in partnership with western professional expertise. People are generally aware of the cultural and language decline but feel a sense of disempowerment. The lack of resources to conduct major work on languages and cultural preservation include the lack of local professional expertise such as linguists for instance, the lack of adequate facilities such as good storage capacity such as libraries, and the lack of financial resources. There is also another major issue and that is the reluctance indigenous people exhibit towards Western professional experts as they are often viewed as exploitative just as much as the national-multinational commercial activities experienced in their own countries.

Participants at a recent UNESCO conference recognized the need to promote a non- biased-mutually beneficial approach to language documentation by both parties; the speech communities and the linguists and the general academic community.

> Any research in endangered language communities must be reciprocal and collaborative. Reciprocity here entails researchers not only offering their services as a quid pro quo for what they received from the speech community, but being more actively involved with the community in designing, implementing, and evaluating their research projects. (UNESCO 2003: 4)

This is the most important but the most neglected issue over centuries of research work particularly in the Third World countries by the western academic community. It is only now in the 21st century, that the issue is beginning to emerge at the international level.

The discussion in the paper is focused on issues and concerns that indicate a sense of urgency in documenting local languages and cultures; the need to preserve such precious cultures and languages in forms that are durable and long lasting. I shall use Bougainville as a case study.

The structure of the paper is as follows:
In the introduction, I muse over two issues. One, is over the definition of 'endanger' or 'endangerment'. At what point does a language becomes threatened of being lost or totally extinct. The other is about the notion, practice and methods of preservation, especially when we consider preserving indigenous cultural and language material with western methods using western resources and facilities. I raise the issue because there are a number of difficulties and problems I imagine that might emerge in the future. For instance, when members of the X speech community in a poor Third World country wish to access their own cultural and

linguistics material stored away in some excellent libraries in Paris or Berlin, and these poor people do not have the financial resources, expertise and technology, how would they be able to access these things?

The second section deals briefly with the development of the vernacular literacy programme for basic early childhood education in Papua New Guinea as the only official form of language and cultural preservation. Following that is the third section, which looks at situations that threatens language and cultural loss. Using Bougainville as a case study, I will discuss not just the threats but also how these threats hasten language and cultural loss. In the final section I shall attempt to discuss what might be some possible solutions to the issue.

What is an endangered language and what does it mean to preserve an endangered language? If it means to preserve an endangered language from complete extinction or one that is facing threats of major loss, what about languages that seem to appear healthy, when in actual fact there has been much deterioration and loss in their cultural contents? Could it be that the word 'endanger' has some level of deception to it? I ponder over the matter because, in my personal work experience in the area since 1980, there are indeed languages that show healthy signs of vitality and yet these languages have lost a substantial amount of cultural contents.

If we are seriously concerned about implementing UNESCO's resolution on protecting biodiversity, cultural and linguistic diversity, we need to reconsider the notion and practice of preserving endangered languages.

In Western countries various forms and ways of language and cultural preservations abound. The situation in the Pacific region is unfortunately lacking, poorly resourced and managed. Western traditional methods of storage, technology and all the relevant facilities and capacities are still way beyond Pacific Island countries' capacity and capability. Western storage places, excellent libraries, institutions, archives and so on are great and continue to serve the West very well, whereas in the Pacific region and in many third world countries such facilities and technology would be quite difficult to access due to the lack of financial resources and expertise available in these countries.

Thousands of speech communities are still by and large oral communities and hence would require alternative approaches appropriate to the situation in language and cultural preservation processes.

How do we tailor language and cultural preservation that would serve the Pacific Island countries better?

2. The development of language preservation in Papua New Guinea (PNG): The Vernacular Literacy Programme in PNG

Local vernacular literacy for basic and early education has been the only officially recognized form of documenting and preserving local languages and cultures in PNG. In the late 1970s and the 1980s, there was a national vernacular programme called, 'the Viles Tok Ples Skul' Programme. It was a two-year vernacular programme for children aged between 6 & 7 years old. After completing these two years, children entered primary school, where English was used as the primary language for instruction and interaction in classrooms and in school grounds. In the 1990s, the national education department of Papua New Guinea introduced what is now called 'the Elementary Schools' system. This is a two year vernacular programme for children before they enter primary schools, whose main language of instruction is English. The elementary school system replaced the Viles Tok Ples Skul (VTPS) Programme (Vernacular Schools). At this point, I do not know much about the changes: why the government felt the need to change or replace VTPS to elementary schools, so I can't comment on the changes. However, many teachers in Bougainville at primary and high school levels are never short of complaints about the new system.

In his paper, 'Language Development in Papua New Guinea', Litteral very briefly touches on UNESCO's advocacy for basic education in local vernaculars as early as the 1950s. The literacy efforts being referred to had been early Christian missionaries' efforts. At this point in time, Papua New Guinea was still under the administration of the Australian government. After independence on September

16, 1975, the national government had a major task at hand. It needed to continue to build and forge national unity in a country that boasts more than 850 local languages and cultures. It soon realized that the most sensible thing to do was to develop or adopt a common national and official language. Pidgin was made the national language, the lexicon of which is composed of 80% English origin and 20% local vernacular languages origin, particularly from the Tolai language of East New Britain. The German language also had some influence in the composition of Pidgin but most of its lexical contributions have died out. Hiri Motu is notionally the other national language although it is mostly spoken around the Port Moresby-Papuan region. English was given official status. It has since been used as the language of education from primary schools right up to the tertiary level, in the media, the parliament, legal institutions, and private and official government offices.

After independence, nation building was very crucial for the newly elected government led by Michael Somare, the first Prime Minister of PNG. People throughout the country had different and conflicting ideas of a PNG national identity. The New Guinea Islands region, particularly the Bougainville and the East New Britain people, could not easily accept an 'overall' PNG identity. The islanders wanted to maintain their distinct languages and cultural identity, rather than be labelled and identified under an imagined national identity, an identity that does not have common cultural and linguistics roots.

Prior to independence during the self-government period (1973-1974), the imagined national identity was already becoming a highly politicized matter. Political agitation was gaining momentum, mostly in Bougainville. The Bougainville people vehemently objected to integration. Important to the people was their cultural identity, and the need to preserve their local languages and cultures.

The Somare government had a major problem to contend with in its early days of running an independent country. From an economic point of view, the national government could not afford to support Bougainville's demand for language and cultural preservation. At the same time, it could not afford to favour one group of people over the other, had it responded to the Bougainville people's wishes. On the other hand, if the government were to take on the task and introduce a nation-wide literacy programme with more than 850 languages and cultures, one wonders what the situation would be like right now. I leave space to the imagination of the reader.

The Papua New Guinea Government's attitude and logic however, failed to convince the people of Bougainville and so in the late 1970s, the people of Bougainville vigorously pursued to fulfil their wishes. This led to the introduction of the Viles Tok Ples Skul (VTPS – a vernacular literacy programme). The scheme was aimed at six to seven year old children immersed in vernacular education in the first two years of initial formal schooling. After graduating, the children entered primary schools where all subjects were taught in English. The English language was also the medium of instruction at primary to tertiary levels nationwide. By 1988, eight out of the 21 major languages in the province had basic literacy materials written and published, including teachers guides. Production of literacy materials ranged from 2,000 to 5,000 copies of each piece of vernacular literature. The estimation was based on the number of children enrolled in VTPS in each speech community. Teachers' guides and other instructional materials and tools were also produced for each VTPS teacher and supervisor.

As the North Solomons Provincial VTPS Coordinator at the time, I felt it was more important to concentrate on the major languages and later deal with the dialects. This solution worked well, as it was quite easy to transfer literacy work done in the major languages to the neighbouring dialects. It was also the most economical way of dealing with numerous dialects in the region. One very important aspect of the VTPS curriculum was the introduction of young and old people as teachers. This was so that both learnt from each other. The young teachers would teach the older teachers modern teaching methods, while the old taught the young ones traditional aspects of culture and custom aimed at children ages six and seven.

The provincial education - VTPS section began work on five additional major languages in 1987 and 1988. Unfortunately the work came to an abrupt end when the armed conflict broke out between the Papua New Guinea Security Forces and the Bougainville Revolutionary Army in early 1989.

In his paper, Litteral refers to this initial effort in introducing local vernaculars for children's initial learning in the North Solomons province in the late 1970s as the first in the nation:

> The awareness of the language issue influenced a university-sponsored survey in the late 1970s in the North Solomons Province, a very politically aware province. The survey showed that parents were concerned about the social alienation of the youth, which they partially blamed on the English education system. They wanted an education that reinforced their language and culture, and at the same time helped their children perform better academically in primary school. A recommendation based on this survey was the basis for the first provincial government policy to support the use of the vernacular for initial literacy and basic education. In 1980 the North Solomons Provincial Government introduced the Viles Tok Ples Skuls (Village Vernacular Schools) program in two languages with an NGO, the Summer Institute of Linguistics (SIL), assisting with materials production and teacher training for literacy. Such was the simple beginning of the post-independence move towards vernacular education, which by 1993 had grown, to over 250 languages (throughout the country). Some policy, accountability and implementation now lay with the communities that received the education. The goal was indigenous development, not westernization. (Litteral 1999: 2)

During the early 1980s, other provinces such as East New Britain, Manus and Enga made visits to the North Solomons Province to observe and learn from the people and the government about the vernacular literacy programmes. Thereafter, these provinces established their vernacular literacy programmes.

Soon other provinces and language communities began vernacular preparatory schools. East New Britain, a highly developed province like the

North Solomons, initiated its program in 1983. Then Enga, a less developed province with the largest vernacular in PNG, began a program in 1985. SIL personnel also assisted both of these provinces. In 1986 the Education Research Unit of the University of PNG began several community-based vernacular programs in Oro Province. Other community-based programs had already begun, primarily with assistance from SIL personnel: Angor in 1981 (Litteral 1999: 2)

Recent UNESCO's analysis of literacy efforts in PNG indicates that, there are over 60 non-government organizations running local literacy programmes, mostly in rural areas and the actual functioning number of literacy classes is estimated to around 5,000. (See UNESCO and the Asia/Pacific Cultural Centre for UNESCO (1997))

The AusAid Country Information web site gives some estimation of the literacy rate between males and females in Papua New Guinea. The 1999 adult literacy rate is 63. 9 per cent of age 15 years old and above, and the female adult literacy rate estimated in 1997 is 56.0 per cent of age 15 years old and above. (See References: AusAid Country Information)

During the eight to ten years armed conflict in the province, all VTPS schools were closed down and or destroyed. They have however, been re-opened as part and parcel the peace process and post-conflict reconstruction and rebuilding. The current approach to literacy vernacular is, however, quite different from the former. The change in the approach also brought with it a change in the label. The current vernacular literacy schools are now called 'elementary' schools. The World Bank, in partnership with the Australian government aid branch AusAID financially supports these schools. Besides these elementary schools, there are other vernacular literacy programmes that are run by local NGOs and most of them are self-supporting. The Inter-Church Women's Forum under the leadership of Sr. Lorraine Garasu runs and supports a children's vernacular programme introduced in January 1998, mostly around the west coast of Bougainville. Sr. Ruby Miringka is not a Catholic Sister, but a former matron as well as a lecturer in the Nursing College in Arawa General Hospital prior to the conflict, who, with the help of other volunteers, established a vernacular literacy programme aimed at children and adults whose education was cut short when the armed conflict broke out.

In summing up this section, the PNG government has shown a great deal of maturity in developing a national policy towards the introduction of vernacular literacy programmes in a nation of more than 850 local languages. Whatever the causes of this historical and political turnabout, PNG has done a great service to its now six million people. Still, there is the need to give adequate attention and resources to documenting large bodies of cultural and linguistic contents in each speech community. It is yet to be seen how far this commitment will go.

3. Bouganville as a case study

3.1. A brief history of Bougainville and the people

The Bougainville people have a colonial history that is characterized by strong resistance to colonial authority and rule, as elsewhere in many Third World countries. If I were to begin with the first European explorer, Louis de Bougainivlle who reached Bougainville on Buka Island in 1768, such contact with outsiders would be currently about 336 years. Other Europeans, including the German New Guinea Company and then the German official administration, entered the region at a much later stage in the early 1880s. From this point on, contact with outsiders was relatively short, about 123 years, yet a time of contact that is smeared with much resistance and objections to external authority and rule.

In a complex set of international relations between Britain, Germany, Australia and the United Nations during the First and Second World War and the post-Second World War period, Bougainville was politically integrated with the rest of Papua New Guinea. Papua New Guinea's independence was declared on September 16, 1975. Meanwhile, two weeks prior to this official occasion, the people and the leaders in Bougainville unilaterally declared their independence. A new set of political dynamics set the tone in the relationship between PNG and the people of Bougainvlle. With the threat to break away from the rest of Papua New Guinea during and after the eve of PNG's independence, a compromise was reached between the two parties. The Bougainvilleans officially declared the provincial government, the first of its kind in the country, in July 1976. The name 'Bougainville' was officially declared the North Solomons and hence, the birth of the North Solomons Provincial Government.

The North Solomons Provincial Government leaders and the public servants managed and governed the province very effectively, and it was one of the most successful provincial government in the country. It was during the North Solomons Provincial Government period (1976 –1988) that the vernacular literacy project was introduced. It was called the 'Viles Tok Ples Skul' (VTPS) Project, a Pidgin label for 'local vernacular literacy schools' or the 'place-talk school' project. It was co-funded and supported by speech communities, the local level governments and the provincial government through the provincial education department. The roles of the speech communities were very vital to the survival and success of the project. The speech communities' support came in varied ways. Members of the communities built teachers' houses and VTPS classrooms from local materials, for instance. Teachers were initially paid in kind by their individual community until they were budgeted for in the over-all provincial VTPS budget allocation in the provincial education department. People made teachers' gardens, brought food to the teachers at scheduled times, mostly fortnightly. Maintenance of teachers' houses and classrooms were also activities in the overall community voluntary support network. During VTPS major language workshops and teachers' training sessions, the local governments' administration provided transportation to and from as well as food for the duration of the workshops and training period. The VTPS central office provided the usual traditional administration and management of the project. Some of the activities include distributing basic school supplies, management of teachers' salaries, plans for language workshops, teachers training and production of literacy materials and many areas.

Returning to the colonial days, while under the control of the Australian administration in the early 1960s, Australian geologists discovered a huge deposit of low-grade copper ore in the mountains of Panguna in Central Boguainville. In 1967, the Australian mining company and the administration signed an agreement to mine the copper ore deposit. The landowners, identified by the name of the mountain as the 'Panguna' landowners, were considered somewhat irrelevant by the administration. The initial mining agreement signed in 1967 between the Australian mining company and the administration made allowance only to compensate the landowners for the destruction of their villages and the natural environment in the area. The agreement stipulated a seven-year period before the agreement could be reviewed.

Complex sets of relationships particularly on economic and political issues dominated and shaped the relationship between the Panguna landowners, the Australian mining company and the Australian administration, the Papua New Guinea government and the North Solomons Provincial Government. By the time the Papua New Guinea government took over from the Australian government at independence, there was already much environmental destruction and pollution being experienced in Bougainville.

The major environmental destruction and pollution comprised some of the long-standing and deep-rooted grievances on the part of the Panguna landowners. Numerous negotiations and peaceful public demonstrations by the Panguna landowners at the North Solomons Provincial government's central administration in in the 1980s went unheeded by the PNG government. By 1988, the young Panguna landowners had become disillusioned. In late 1988, young men blew up a couple of electrical pylons along the Panguna highway that connected the mine site to the mine port. This action got the PNG national government's attention. It sent in its police riot squad to contain the unrest. The PNG police riot squad's behaviour was unbecoming. There were unwarranted killings of civilians, raping of women, military-style interrogation of young men suspected of supporting the conflict, burning down village houses, killing domestic animals and general intimidation and harassment of the landowners and the general population in the immediate vicinity of the mine site. In response to this aggressive uncontrolled behaviour, the young men regrouped properly in order to protect and defend their mothers, fathers, brothers, sisters and children and their land. The young men put up strong resistance against the riot squad under the label the 'Bougainville Revolutionary Army' (BRA). To break the strong resistance from the BRA, the PNG government deployed its Defence Force troops as reinforcement of its security forces in Arawa, where they set up their base. With the combined forces meeting a small local force, the conflict escalated. Fighting spread throughout Bougainville as soon as the course of the conflict took on a new cloak from purely an economic one to political independence. According to the young men, the fight was now over Bougainville's independence, a total and complete breakaway from the rest of Papua New Guinea. The PNG Security Forces recruited young men who became the local militia under the name the 'Bougainville Resistance Force' (BLF). The armed conflict escalated in early 1989 and lasted through to 1997. In addition, the national government imposed a complete blockade in the region. The people were blockaded from receiving normal government services at the time; except for the intervention of the international community, there was little help coming in. The conflict resulted in an estimation of 15,000 to 18,000 to 20,000 people who have lost their lives. These figures need to be verified as yet.

Through the help of the international community in peace monitoring duties and activities in the Bougainville peace process, mainly by the New Zealand, Australian, Fijian and Vanuatu governments, it became possible for Bougainville and Papua New Guinea to negotiate a settlement. In July of the year 2001, the Bougainville leaders including the leaders of the local warring factions and the PNG Government officials signed the Bougainville Agreement witnessed by representatives from the United Nations Office and the New Zealand, Australian, Fiji and Vanuatu governments. The Agreement is yet again another power-sharing compromise, though there is more power given to the people than with the previous provincial government system. In the Agreement, Bougainville is now called, the 'Bougainville Autonomous Region' and the government the, 'Bougainville Autonomous Government'. It has its own constitution and will have some degree of dealing directly with the international community.

3.2 The impact of the armed conflict on Indigenous languages, cultures and customs

During the period of the armed conflict and the economic blockade, the majority of the population turned to the environment and the forest for food, shelter, and for medicine and to God for protection.

I wish to quote one of the most outstanding community programmes set up by dedicated Bougainvilleans who managed to maintain their community during the most difficult time of the armed conflict in the jungle of Central Bougainville. The programme's primary objective was to integrate modern and traditional ideas and practices. Sister Ruby Miringka(1996), who is a professional trained nurse and a health lecturer, describes the programme as follows:

> Despite the traumas of the war and deprivation of people's basic right to life, health care, education, shelter, security and right to self-determination, the civilians in the non-government-controlled areas have become determined not to sit idle and wait for a rescue mission from somewhere but rather we would use our community and resources within the community to bring about development, in attempts to alleviate the sufferings and that of our people from common preventable diseases.
>
> Further [we aim] to bring about social changes that would encourage community participation, through activities and projects promoting healthy living and education to promote self-reliance and survival within a war environment.
>
> (Miringka 1996: 52-54)

The Community Development Programme began with the formation of Village Health Committees in selected villages of Central Bougainville.

Most of the trainees were highly qualified doctors, nurses and teachers who were now living in the jungle with the people. Sr. Ruby Miringka, who was one of the most prominent figures in the programme is a highly qualified nursing sister and was one of the lecturers in the former Arawa General Hospital. The trainers were paid in kind: each community made food gardens, brought food and provided coconut oil used for cooking, lamps and to run vehicles.

A second major component of the programme was an experiment in combining both local and modern skills and practices appropriate for village community based life style, such as traditional midwifery, medicine, old-age and disabled care, and post-traumatic counselling.

This is an exciting programme based on a holistic approach combining both traditional and modern ways of dealing with life. However, considering the number of people that have lost their lives during the armed conflict, thousands of them are old people and hence, thousands of whole rich traditional libraries have been lost forever. What Sr. Miringka and her people have tried to retrieve is a rather unfortunate late effort but at least an attempt. These efforts had fortunately sustained civilians living in the jungle without medical supplies and many other forms of assistance during the period of the conflict from 1989 to 1997 and even through to the year 2000 as people were afraid to come out from hiding.

3.3 Effects of large-scale multinational companies on indigenous languages, cultures and customs

We have found the same situation with the impact of the mining activities on languages and customs. One might ask the question, how do large-scale multinational mining and logging activities fast track the process of language and cultural loss or how are they a big threat to the survival of cultures and languages?

Large-scale environmental damage and destruction result in the loss of large bodies that have cultural and language contents. Lost forever are: floral and fauna; rivers and living creatures in river systems; virgin forests with rich biodiversity; birds species; special species of plants and trees that are of medicinal and cultural values. When such life systems are gone, so too is the language content gone forever.

The biodiversity, the ecology of the place, traditional cosmology and the cultural and linguistics richness of the environment, the spirituality of the place, all these have been substantially lost. In many ways, Bougainvilleans are trying to salvage what is left of the cultural and language life today.

3.4 The deception of a healthy language: misleading and potential threats to language and cultural loss

During the pre-armed conflict period, from 1980 to 1988, I worked with the North Solomons Provincial Government's Literacy Project. My husband and I left the island in early January 1990 for Australia. Over the years during the period of the conflict, I was able to visit my family, the people and friends on the island. During these visits, I continued to document the Teop language in the Teop speech community in northeast Bougainville. Although my mother spoke a different language to my father's, which is the Teop language, I grew up speaking the two languages. Documenting the Teop language has given me immense pleasure and an enjoyment of my father's culture as never before. In the meantime, I had the nagging feeling that, most people of my age group probably do not know the cultural and language material I was now learning from a few old people who are still alive. If that were the case, then the younger generations are left in a far worse cultural poverty situation. I then decided to carry out a little test to test my assumption.

4. Testing my assumption

The crowd I gathered included grades four and five and six of Kekesu primary school children, one of the major primary schools in the speech community. I also included two elementary classes (kindergarten level using local vernacular as the medium of instruction and as a subject) and a reasonably sized group of old and elderly people, both male and female. I also included a group of people of my age group.

I played a few CDs containing some of the interviews. In between each interview, I asked rather simple questions. I had selected subjects or particular cultural matters, which I was learning at the time of the interviews on which I based the questions.

I selected these because I thought, if I did not know them, then those in my age group would also not know them. In the case of the children, they wouldn't have the slightest clue. In marine life, I picked a few fish species; their names, habitat, feeding and breeding times that I had just learnt. In traditional fishing technology and methods of fishing, I applied the same technique. I asked the young men how many of them knew what is involved in making fishing kites and how they are used and where in the sea. I also designed questions specifically for women in their activities and roles in fishing and other related areas. The questions I asked were based on some of the materials I have collected in these areas:

- knowledge of marine life; species and names of fish in shallow and deep sea; fishing gear; fishing methods;
- traditional fishing gear and fishing methods including fishing nets and kites.
- canoe making and carving paddles and punts with relevant traditional ceremonies.
- house-building; names of trees used in house-building; the stages involved in house-building;
- initiation ceremonies for young boys and girls;
- engagement and marriage;
- women's activities in mat and basket weaving; fishing and gardening.
- children's songs and games and dances;
- personal history of people's experiences in the Second World War and of early local pioneers who assisted in ushering in modern development and Christianity.

I was pleasantly surprised that my hypothesis proved positive and negative. On the positive side, my test case showed that, all the young people and people in their 40s lack considerable cultural knowledge and skills. On the truly negative side, there is indeed a high level of deception in believing that, if people live in the cultural environment, where there is cultural savvy all around them, there is the assumption and expectation that living live cultures truly entrench people in the culture. On the contrary, that is not true. It is a widely held perception and unfortunately, it is highly misleading. On the basis of the result of the test, I was satisfied to know that the problem is widespread.

5. Vernacular literacy in basic education cannot deliver all the goods.
Reflecting on my involvement in language and cultural preservation and maintenance with a very strong streak to maintain them in the liveliest forms, I am now having to re-adjust my position from basic education in local vernaculars to much, much more substantial and intensive work. The input from cultural and language studies has to make up a reasonable component of the school curriculum. PNG's general literacy policy, one that states that vernacular literacy would not just be about reading and writing but also about learning, thinking, critiquing and expanding vision; and about a desire for life-long learning in all Papua New Guineans and equipping them with the skills to fulfil that desire. If that is to be followed through, the national government and all the respective departments must seriously consider elevating the status of early vernacular literacy to an advanced status. The advanced body of cultural and language subjects would meet the intellectual needs of the students at primary school and high school levels. At the moment the efforts are very minimal and very basic.

The UNESCO proposed action plan recommended that Member States, in conjunction with speech communities, undertake steps to ensure:

1. sustaining the linguistic diversity of humanity and giving support to expression, creation, and dissemination of the greatest possible number of languages;
2. encouraging linguistic diversity at all levels of education, wherever possible, and fostering the learning of several languages from the youngest age;
3. incorporating, where appropriate, traditional pedagogies into the education process with a view to preserving and making full use of culturally-appropriate methods of communication and transmission of knowledge; and where permitted by speaker communities, encouraging universal access

to information the public domain through the global network, including linguistic diversity in cyberspace. (UNESCO 2003: 5)

These are very heartening steps although at times, the reality is often very discouraging, particularly when respective governments do not pay attention to these sorts of pro-active measures to preserve languages and cultures.

5.1 Western forms of preservation of local languages and cultures could become a major problem.

There are a number of major problems, if we are to preserve local languages, cultures and customs mostly in the western ways of preservation. By preserving these in Western ways, I am referring to advanced technological ways of preservation; through CDs, on the Internet, in libraries and other institutions.

The problem I find here is that the speech communities in Third World countries do not have the resources and expertise to access their very own languages, cultures and customs stored in excellent conditions in far away places, mostly in western countries. How can a simple villager access his stored-away well-preserved language and culture in CDs in some excellent library in France or Germany for instance? What local expertise is available to help the poor fellow access his materials on the Internet, for instance? What financial assistance does he have access to in order to access his own language and culture well preserved in overseas countries?

If we were to take this approach in language preservation then, essentially in my view, this form of preservation would only assist in the gradual decline of the languages, cultures and customs.

6. Solutions?

Preservation is the way to go but must be accompanied with most lively forms of approach to language preservation to serve speech communities that are still largely oral, and that do not have all the resources and expertise.

The barefoot linguist concept is the best approach so far as proposed by linguists from Papua New Guinea and West Papua (formerly Irian Jaya).

The barefoot linguists idea is about training members of speech communities to become '........ linguistic fieldworkers rather than highly trained theoretical linguists. What is needed in these regions now, is not so much linguists who collect their data in the field and leave to write an academic piece, but people who can provide language communities with an alphabet and an outline of the grammar...." (See References: UNESCO (1997))

In September 1995, from 28 August to 2nd September, the first international conference on New Guinea Languages and Linguistics' conference was held at the University of Cenderawasih in Jayapura. The Universities of Cenderawasih in Jayapura and Papua New Guinea (PNG) jointly organized the conference. Participants came from seven different countries and it was the first of its kind between Jayapura and Port Moresby. The discussion at the conference focused on '.... data from languages on both sides of the border and ... ... efforts to safeguard the declining or dying languages in the two regions.' Papua New Guinea vernacular languages number around less than a thousand languages, an estimated one fifth of world's languages. Many of these have fewer than 5,000 speakers, and some as few as 500 or less. ... . Many of these languages are still largely unknown and unwritten.
(See References: UNESCO (1997))

This is a very encouraging development, particularly for Papua New Guinea with its cultural and linguistics diversity.

But the question remains, how do we preserve languages and cultures in the liveliest forms, catering for the purposes and needs of mostly oral speech communities?

Because I am a proponent of keeping languages alive and well, it would be important for people like us to help local people define the sorts of practical activities that would be helpful for them. One these pro-active activities would be theatre. Theatrical activities would best suit local communities in Third World countries as most of their learning processes are through imitation. Another that comes to mind is through media-particularly audio-visual media such as videos.

Note

1. I read this paper at the International Expert Meeting on Endangered Languages, Paris, France on March 10-12th 2003.

References

AusAid Country Information (n.d.) About Papua New Guinea. (n.d.) http://www.ausaid.gov.au/country/png/png_intro.cfm Accessed 25/02/2003.

Litteral, R. (1999) Language development in Papua New Guinea. SIL Electronic Working Papers, 1999-002, February 1999. http://www.sil.org.sileqp/1999/002/SILEWP1999-002.html Accessed 07/07/2006.

Miringka, R. (1996) *Women speak out on Bougainville*. Community Development Program. Forum Papers, pp. 52-54.

Quodling, P. (1991) *Bougainville: The Mine and the People*. St Leonards, NSW, Centre for Independent Studies, *Pacific Papers* No.3.

UNESCO and the Asia/Pacific Cultural Centre for UNESCO (1997) National Literacy Policies: Papua New Guinea http://www.accu.or.jp/litdbase/policy/png/Accessed 25/02/2003.

UNESCO (2003) Language Vitality and Endangerment: UNESCO Ad Hoc ExpertGroup on Endangered Languages. http://portal.unesco.org/culture/en/file_download.php/4794680ecb5664addb9af1234a4a1839Language+Vitality+and+Endangerment.pdf.

The Role of Lingua Francas in Papua New Guinea[1]

Daniel K. Leke
University of Papua New Guinea

1. Introduction

This chapter takes the form of a literature review on the issue of language and education in Papua New Guinea, focusing on the three main lingua francas: *English, Tok Pisin and Hiri Motu* and how they have played and could play their roles in the educational development of the country.[2] At the outset, one considers it necessary to provide an operational definition of the three lingua francas, followed by providing a conceptual framework and an overview of the country, early European contact, and linguistic trends, including early developments and related colonial and current language policies.

Then we look at general education developments and the place of language, mainly drawing on the ideological principles derived from the PNG Philosophy of Education and the place of language in the current education system. The final section deals with the extent to which the lingua francas (mainly English and Tok Pisin) have played or could play their roles in educational development in both formal and informal settings in the country. The discussion is concluded with a brief summary highlighting the position of the English language in Papua New Guinea.

2. Definitions of the three lingua francas and early developments

The main lingua francas in Papua New Guinea include: *English*, *Tok Pisin* and *Hiri Motu*. *Lingua franca* refers to a language that is nobody's mother tongue or first language. It is a common language that enables communication among speakers of Papua New Guinea's many other languages. The English lingua franca is used as an official language in the country, while Tok Pisin and Hiri Motu have remained un-official, although they actually do have official roles in education and in the Constitution today.

The English language entered the shores of Port Moresby with its British speakers around 1870s and subsequently, the British and the local people were using it as a 'broken form' of English or Pidgin language. For example, the Rev. W.G. Lawes of the London Missionary Society settled in Port Moresby in 1874 as the first European missionary among the Motuans and was using a broken form of English to communicate with the people (Piau, Lynch and Crowley in Lynch, 1992: 113). A broken form of English was also introduced by native labourers returning from work experience in Queensland, Australia. This was reinforced by the British Administration under the first Governor –Sir William MacGregor in 1888 up until a full version of the 'pure' English language was administered by the British in 1897. The policy of English as the official language of government was maintained later by the Australians under their protectorate from 1906 onwards (Piau, Lynch and Crowley in Lynch, 1992: 115).

'Tok Pisin' is simply 'Pidgin Talk' in English, which really is an English-based Pidgin (with a few German and native word features) used in Papua New Guinea and other nearby island nations, including Solomon Islands, Vanuatu and Fiji with various varieties. Hudson (1990: 64) has examined the development and use of Tok Pisin and revealed that the lingua franca has developed effectively and become accepted as a medium of communication in so many domains and recently has turned into a creole language. The language has acquired native speakers in parts of the New Guinea Islands and Momase regions.

The third lingua franca is 'Hiri Motu' and it is spoken by people who live along the coast of the southern part of the country who are referred to as the 'Papuans'. This pidgin language has derived from indigenous languages around that area for the purpose of communicating with colonial police personnel present in the area. Piau, Lynch and Crowley, in Lynch (1992: 111) and Kale, in Baldauf and Luke (1990: 184) in their findings, showed that this lingua franca was known then as *'Police Motu'* because it was used to communicate with policemen during the colonial administration. However, today, it is recognized as 'Hiri Motu' because the people used this lingua franca at the arrival of colonialism along the coastal areas from the 'Gulf of Papua'(today's Gulf Province) to 'Hanuabada' (today's Port Moresby). Unlike the English and Tok Pisin lingua francas that play important roles nationally, Hiri Motu tends to play a restricted role today.

It seems that in the colonial period, Hiri Motu and Tok Pisin lingua francas played significant roles between the colonizers and natives, especially in relation to communication. English was seen to be indirectly introduced, initially through the form of broken English (Pidgin) but eventually, the colonial administrators felt that it was necessary for their mother tongue to be taught not only as a pidgin variety but as pure English. This change came about as a result of language policy which we shall explore a bit more later in this chapter.

3. Conceptual framework

When looking at linguistic aspects of education from a humanistic sociological, conflict and functionalist perspectives in the case of Papua New Guinea, one is challenged to rediscover the significant roles that language plays. The humanistic sociological perspective tends to argue that, all actions (of whatever sort) are (or should be) seen and interpreted from the actor's point of view (Zaniecki, 1982: 10). Smolicz (1979: 22) elaborates this perspective and maintains that, one's observation of social, cultural or behavioural forms should be in line with the way in which they function in the consciousness of the people who produce and maintain them.

The role of language in this regard, is valued in any society and when seen from a humanistic sociological perspective, is very crucial because it expresses people's thoughts, feelings, values and belief systems. It also enforces rules, gives direction and expresses its speakers' hopes and aspirations. Language is the means through which verbal and written information is passed on between individuals or groups who may speak one or more languages. Therefore, one has to know the language of the other in order to understand its related cultural and philosophical issues that are imbedded in that language. Without such understanding, communication becomes a problem.

Such lack of understanding of one another's language, especially in the context of Papua New Guinea, seems to become a barrier for effective communication, thus resulting in linguistic-related conflicts. One would view that conflict (of whatever sort) is something that can be seen in every society where individuals or groups compete with each other for the purpose of gaining prestige, wealth and power. These struggles can usually result either in creating group solidarity (cohesion) or disintegrate harmony in society.

When relating this conflict theory to the issue of language, media and information packaging in PNG, it is seen to be controlled by those in power in the bureaucratic level. They decide what language is to be used in government, education, science, technology, commerce and media. These people have their own political agendas and objectives to be achieved through the use of a language of their choice, especially the English medium. In their endeavour to achieve these ends, they tend to provide no chance for the so-called 'grass-roots' who are in fact, the majority of the population who speak well over 850 languages, including the two lingua francas (Tok Pisin and Hiri Motu). As a result, there seems to be a creation of inequality in communication and information consumption among the elite group and the ordinary Papua New Guineans. Further, the decision-makers are failing to see the fact that all languages, including the three lingua francas, are very crucial for the effective functioning and maintenance of multilingual Papua New Guinea and its culture. It is the language that makes individuals as active human agents, not only in communication but also in preserving and maintaining the culture and other structures of life in PNG society.

As such, Smolicz (1992: 7) argues that language is a core value, a carrier of culture, plays the role as a bridge for intercultural communication and becomes an identity marker for the group. Hernandez-Chavez, in Skuddnabb-Kangas and Cummins (1988: 45) discusses language policy and language rights in the United States and argues that language on the cultural level is seen to be the symbolic expression of the community, encoding a group's value, its folklore and its history. In this sense, language is the most powerful means of interaction and communication in order for individuals or groups to participate equally in society.

Foster (1981: 11) further analyses society from the structural functionalist perspective and argues that society is structured and functions in such a way that suits people who belong to it. As such, the function of language in society is important because it is structured and shared by people who belong to a social group whose members wish to communicate with one another. Without proper understanding or insufficient knowledge of a language, attempts at communication tend to result in misunderstandings, which sometimes lead to conflicts or broken relationships. When looking at linguistic-related conflicts generally, they may develop among a community in which a multiple number of languages are spoken.

In societies where some languages are dominant among other minority languages, there tends to be an overlap where the dominant language plays a higher role – usually restricted to the particular ethnic community. The dominant language can be used by a majority group of people from certain ethnic or linguistic background because it is either their mother tongue or is a language of prestige, of trade, law, medicine, education and international media. It is also becoming a language of instruction, science and technology and international communication in the Third World countries (including Papua New Guinea) that have previously been colonized by Britain, Australia and the United States of America.

As far as its speakers are concerned, as the *Times of Papua New Guinea* (1995: 8) puts it, English is used today by more than one billion people worldwide, of whom half have learned it as a second (or third) language. According to Barbara

Dieu (2005) of the English Department at Sao Paulo, Brazil, there are at least seventy-five countries with a total population of over two billion who speak English as either native language (375 million) or as a second language by around 375 million. And speakers of English as second language will soon outnumber those who speak it as first language. Around 750 million people are believed to speak English as a foreign language. One out of four of the world's population, speak English to some level of competence. Demand from the other three-quarters is increasing.

4. English language monopoly in Papua New Guinea

It becomes a concern when a dominant language becomes superior among the minority ones. It tends to over-power the minority ones and takes the lead in educational, social political, economic and other aspects of life. As a result of this domination, the minority languages become threatened and therefore, the speakers of these minority languages are indirectly being deprived of their right to know and maintain those languages. Thus, most of the people are being influenced to learn and use the dominant language. When this process occurs, they tend to loose interest in their own minority languages and the tendency to activate and maintain them becomes secondary. Minority languages then exist around the periphery and may eventually die if there is no revival of interest among those who can speak them (Smolicz, 1979: 9).

Such linguistic dilemma is seen to be prevalent in Papua New Guinea where the English language is becoming dominant among other lingua francas and minority languages. It is dominant because of its recognition by the national government and because of the fact that it is used as a medium of communication in all sectors of life in the country. At the community level however, Tok Pisin is seen to be dominant and is spreading widely (also refer Roebuck, in Thirlwall and Hughes, 1989: 39). Tok Pisin, of course, is dominant and is seen to be "a thriving living language" (Palmer, in *Post-Courier*, Wednesday May 10, 1995: 11).

Most of the written forms of communication available in the country seem to be in the English language, to which most Papua New Guineans have limited access. The written and spoken information in the English code being transmitted across the country among diversified linguistic and cultural lines is considered to be wasteful because most people do not understand the language (Nekitel and Kamene, 1991: 2). Most of the government or official information available is consumed by a minority group of urban settlers who have access to that language because of their educational background.

Moreover, one may argue that because Papua New Guinea has more than 850 languages (Nekitel and Kamene, 1991: 3), intercultural communication would become a problem and that English should remain as official because it would play a neutral role in bringing about cultural integration and development. Such an ideological assumption is seen to be related to the colonial policy-makers' view that has led to the adoption if the English-only policy, thus indicating that the English language would play a neutral role in multilingual Papua New Guinea. Whatever the ideology behind the policy, one should not think that this is necessarily the best or only solution to the linguistic problems the country faces today.

One could argue that adopting a foreign language (English) as a medium of communication in an ethnically plural society (as in the case of Papua New Guinea), where other lingua francas and vernacular languages are dominant, would not easily alleviate the linguistic-related problems. English could not properly represent Papua New Guinea culture and play an active role in bringing about effective cultural integration and maintenance. The English language, however, would be seen as a bridge for promoting and maintaining the value systems of those societies (especially Europeans) in Papua New Guinea.

When talking about 'minding your language' (*The Times of Papua New Guinea*, February 23, 1995: 8), the writer sees the English-only policy in the country as linguistic imperialism, which tends to contribute to the disempowerment of the people denied access to it and the devaluation of other native languages. This statement is seen to be valid because when looking at the role of language from a Papua New Guinean perspective, the English language is an imperial language that seems to be playing some roles in scientific and technological life and development, but not solely for the best interest of the majority of people in the country and their culture.

It appears that the English language has monopoly over educational, economic, political and other aspects of life and as such, only a minority group of people are getting most of its benefits. The provision of vital government or other information and the majority's right to know and become competent in an already existing community language (lingua franca) in order to participate and become effective members as of society multicultural Papua New Guineans, is perceived to be somewhat limited.

4.1 Language policies in Papua New Guinea

Papua New Guinea got its political independence from Australia in 1975 and yet the importance of a national language policy was then not on the national government's political agenda. Under both the British and Australian administration, the language policy was in favour of the colonizers' mother tongue regardless of Tok Pisin and Hiri Motu, which had gained some strength in the community. Without much further consideration and consultation with the people of PNG concerning the possibility of accommodating one or both of the lingua francas (Tok Pisin and Hiri Motu), "the PNG government had inherited the English only legacy of its colonizers" (Nekitel, 1984: 8) as an official lingua franca for Papua New Guinea. It could be argued that there should have been a more lenient or flexible language policy which would have accommodated both English and Tok Pisin (or Hiri Motu). This was seen to be not the case for the country after independence in 1975.

If one can refer to language policies elsewhere, especially countries in the Southeast Asia and African regions, it is seen that most of these countries have gone through language reforms after political independence from their former colonizers. For example, Nekitel (1989: 124) identifies the fact that, there was a linguistic and literacy revolution taking place in India, Malaysia, Indonesia, Philippines, Tanzania and so on, where these countries saw the need for their non-metropolitan national and official languages to become enriched with scientific and technical terms to enable them to become more effective tools of communication in their fast-changing societies.

Many of these nations, however, gave serious thought to adopting their indigenous lingua francas, such as Bahasa Malaysia or Bahasa Indonesia, Pilipino (formerly Tagalog), Hindi in India or Swahili in Tanzania and borrow scientific and technical terms from the languages of their former imperial powers (Nekitel, 1989: 124). Previous studies done by Johnson (1974: 24) have also shown that the above stated nations, as well as Sri Lanka, Pakistan and Bangladesh had adopted English as the medium of instruction, but later on, this policy was abandoned for primary education at least. Moreover, countries such as Zambia, Kenya, Ethiopia and a number of West African nations have reintroduced or are introducing vernacular education in the lower grades.

These countries, although multilingual in nature, seemed to have accommodated their major local lingua francas in government. In the case of Papua New Guinea, although Tok Pisin, Hiri Motu and the other native languages seemed to have played some vital roles, especially the majority's knowledge of them, the national government failed to give any consideration to giving them official status at the national level. When responding to the national language policy debate in parliament after Independence in 1975, Sir Michael Somare, then Chief Minister, stated that, "English would probably be the official language for administration while Tok Pisin and Hiri Motu could be the official languages for other purposes" (Piau, Lynch and Crowley, in Lynch, 1992: 136).

It seems that such statement by a Chief Minister at that time, supporting the 'status quo' of the former British and Australian colonial language policy, was not questioned and debated by other politicians at that time. The language issue, especially in relation to Tok Pisin and Hiri Motu, "was not debated in the Floor of Parliament or clearly stated in the National Constitution although, the knowledge of one or the other or both is one of the indispensable prerequisites for granting of citizenship by naturalization" (Nekitel, 1989: 130). One assumes four possible reasons for the national government's indecisiveness in giving a thought to language planning in Papua New Guinea.

Firstly, perhaps the government was being misled by the colonial language policy that was in place by thinking that English is 'the only language' that would solve the linguistic and other social problems in the country by bringing about integration and development at both local and national levels.

Secondly, the government perhaps was possibly in fear that it did not have the financial and manpower capability to get the language policy started and implemented.

Thirdly, the government feared that any new language adopted as a national (or official) lingua franca could perhaps take the place of the English language, thus resulting in the under-development of the country by international standards.

Finally, the government perhaps believed that the other two lingua francas in the country (Tok Pisin and Hiri Motu) are more limited than English in terms of vocabulary or grammatical structures and therefore, restrict access to and narrow the vital scientific and technical knowledge and skills required for society today.

It could be argued that if these were the perceived reasons for not having a clear language policy by the national government, then it failed. The national government should see what other countries in the Asia-Pacific region have done where language planning and development have become central in their government agendas. Nations such as Japan, China, South and North Korea, Malaysia, or PNG's closest neighbour – Indonesia, as well as those other Asian and African countries mentioned earlier, are seen to be developing politically, economically and socially more rapidly. They have studied and borrowed scientific and technical terms from their former colonial powers (if they were colonized by any foreign power) and developed their own linguistic systems in order to meet their own cultural, economical, political and other educational needs.

There seems to be no good reason why Papua New Guinea should be an exception. In fact, the country does have two existing dominant lingua francas (Tok Pisin and English) and if the government were to develop a language policy by making the Tok Pisin lingua franca official, then it could borrow scientific and technical terms from the metropolitan (English) language without much difficulty. Tok Pisin in this respect has a greater advantage than Hiri Motu because most of its words have been derived from the English language and also it is spoken today by most Papua New Guineans.

4.2 The place of language in the philosophy of education in PNG

Papua New Guinea's present education system is seen to be based on an ideology which has been derived wholly from the Philosophy of Education Policy document. The philosophy calls for the development of the whole person (i.e., integral human development). This means that education should be geared towards integrating and maximizing the potential of individuals' their socialization, participation, liberation, and equality (Ministerial Committee Report, 1986: 7). The report further elaborates this philosophy by indicating that, in order to achieve the goals of socialization, the children must be first provided with an opportunity to become dynamically involved with others in family contexts, church, community, and beyond. The implication of this in relation to language is that, if language is narrowly seen here as a socializing agent, only vernacular languages should be used as a medium of instruction initially at primary level, at least in the first two years. This same ideology was also emphasized and maintained in the 1991 Education Sector Review. Yet, neither of these documents explicitly discusses which language is to be used as the means of instruction.

Furthermore, the Philosophy of Education seems to explain the children's need for a holistic approach to education and development in Papua New Guinea. However, it seems that the Philosophy does not clearly identify the significance of language, which is viewed by others as the carrier of cultural values or as an identity marker (Smolicz, 1992: 7). One can, in principle, agree with the four goals of education: socialization, participation, liberation and equality. However, the question one may ask is how? How would the stated goals be achieved through a foreign language if the "majority of the population are illiterate in English" (Nekitel and Kamene, 1991: 4)?

Teaching in English, learning it as a core subject and using it in a school situation for the bilingual and multilingual children in PNG would not meet those goals effectively because English is still seen to be a foreign language. Without true proficiency in the country's unofficial lingua francas (Tok Pisin and Hiri Motu), socialization, participation, interaction, skill sharing and transmission of cultural knowledge and value systems to a much deeper and meaningful level, is seen as meaningless and can not materialize fully, although local languages and often the two major lingua francas are now the medium of education in early primary school in Papua New Guinea. The retaining of English as the official medium of instruction and communication is a direct contradiction to the ideology of liberation from oppression as stipulated in the Philosophy. Given the linguistic diversity in the country, it should not be assumed that integral human development would come automatically by allowing an imposed foreign language to be used as the only means of instruction and communication for the people of Papua New Guinea.

It appears therefore, that PNG is yet to be liberated from the linguistic, economic and political domination of colonial culture. Linguistic liberation in this sense means that the people use either Tok Pisin or Hiri Motu as official languages rather than English, which currently can be shown to be enslaving the majority from getting information or sharing information equally. Economic liberation is still a question because at the moment most of the country's economy is owned and run by foreign multinational corporations (mostly speaking English). Most technological innovation is yet to materialize in the country. In fact, the English language associated with this technology is difficult for a semi-English literate to comprehend. Political liberation in the narrower sense is evident but it appears that most of the decisions regarding the nation's economy are determined by those in power and the foreign capitalists who own the means of production and for whom English is their common language.

5. Packaging and dissemination of public information in Papua New Guinea

As the official language in Papua New Guinea, English is used in the classroom, in the office, in the national parliament, in media, in the courts, in diplomatic missions, and in other business transactions. Most vital information the people ought to know is usually made available in print and electronic media via English. Important information such as the national constitution is written in the English language. There has been a Tok Pisin version of the national constitution only since the 1990s. Most bank details, company contract documents, legal documents, health-related documents, such as the information about HIV/AIDS that most people need to know and be aware are written in the English language.

Regarding language and media, Nekitel and Kamene (1991: 1-3) describe the current situation and how the lingua francas contribute to educational development, especially in rural areas of the country. They discuss the fact that the country has become an integral member of the global community and as such, it has adapted and will continue to adapt to communication media that will facilitate and bolster up its communication needs and demands expected of a modern thriving nation. The authors also see the importance of communication in all walks of life through the use of various modes of communication relevant to the local and international community. They further maintain that official information was entertained or consumed by only 20 percent of the people who live in urban areas of the country. The information does not reach out to rural centres where the bulk of the country's population (80 percent), most of whom are illiterate in the English language, actually live.

The two national newspapers ('Post-Courier' and 'The National') are written in the English language. The only television in the country (EMTV) has the main news being read in the English language; this is not mentioning the whole variety of foreign programmes relayed or played in the English language. The National Broadcasting Commission (NBC) has never been monolingual. Tok Pisin news has always been there, and today there are stations broadcasting solely in Tok Pisin, both at the regional and national levels. Most of this information being presented through the English medium is consumed by the 20 percent of people living in urban areas of the country and do not reach out to the majority of the people who live in rural areas of the country.

Concerning this information consumption scenario, Gillian, in Thirlwall and Hughes (1989: 1) argues that, information packaging and dissemination in Papua New Guinea is not in the best interest of the majority but of the minority, and in most cases, of the foreign capitalists who have business interests in the country. This means that information technology is selected and transmitted in such a way that only those in power and the foreigners can benefit. The author highlights the fact that multinational corporations tend to control communication technology, such as television, satellites, computer networks and other non-electronic media publications. The media owners decide what information is relevant, not only for the people but for the media owners' own interests.

The language use in these electronic and print media tends to be selected very carefully so that only the privileged ones can understand and interpret the information presented. For the purpose of product marketing and health-related awareness campaigns, such as condom use, only a limited amount of Tok Pisin is used. Such development in the country seems to show that self-reliance in communication is not effective because most people are only receivers of the information from the top down. One would therefore, agree with the editorial published by the National Language Project of South Africa (Siegruhn, 1994) regarding the part that language plays in national development. This article states that, unless the role of language is clearly articulated and integrated in a cross-sector growth plan, the country could lose out on crucial human resources in economic development. Any attempt to redress inequality and lack of access to sectors such as health care and justice will remain solely at the level of intent, if inadequate language services continue to function.

Such concerns for linguistic inequality in South African and other African cases are also prevalent in Papua New Guinea. Although some mission organizations do attempt to teach literacy skills to adults, especially women, for the purpose of reading religious texts and getting better information about health and hygiene, the national government has done little in providing such information in a language that most people know and speak. Therefore, it appears that self-reliance and true participation in encoding and efficient decoding of public information and awareness in a common language in Papua New Guinea appear to be limited.

5.1 Students and professionals lacking English skills

Linguistic equality in the formal and informal settings in relation to learning and use seems to be somewhat limited. Communication and information access is restricted to a few people who are literate in the English language. In the school system, however, it has been found that, as a result of the English-only policy, most students fail tests and exams taken in the English language (Nekitel, 1991: 133 and Education Sector Review, 1991: 3). Also, one academic at the University of Papua New Guinea saw most students at the University performing poorly in their expression in English when essays were written in different subject areas. He therefore blames PNG teachers in primary and secondary schools, whose English is either their second or third language, for passing on their inadequate knowledge of the English language to students (*Post-Courier*, Thursday June 29, 1995: 10).

The above information can be verified by recent essays from students ranging from first to fourth years at the University of Papua New Guinea. It was shown that most students who have handed in the essays were found to have difficulty in expressing ideas coherently and logically. Wordy and redundant phrases were used without thought and simple words were misused and applied in wrong contexts. Some students do not seem to differentiate terms such as 'about/approximately', 'accept/except', 'advise/inform', 'affect/effect', 'because of/due to', 'can/may', convince/persuade' or 'who/whom'.

This is not to mention the common fallacies that students fall into when writing and speaking in English. Maybe the students' thinking process is shaped by their own language and cultural upbringing. This can be shown in student writings where there tend to be problems with consistency, correlation of ideas, subject/verb agreements and other requirements of formal writing. If students at the University of Papua New Guinea are seen to be making such mistakes in the English language, one wonders if there are not more students out there in colleges and universities across the country finding the English lingua franca hard.

Similarly, Parker (1986: 42) noticed serious problems when he ran a series of English courses for people who have professional positions. In summary, the results of running this courses showed that most students simply do not know English competently, or they know and speak quite accurate English but their pronunciation, intonation, stress placement, lack of full knowledge and difficulty in expression were problems. The author noticed that the accent in the English language had been influenced or interfered with either by their own language or the Tok Pisin. For example, English words with similar sounds like – 'sack' and 'shack' or 'tank' and 'thank' which when used or pronounced by students sounded like, 'sek' and 'sek' or 'tenk' and 'tenk' in Tok Pisin. Such differences in the sound system were noticed because the Tok Pisin language does not have a number of consonant sounds present in English such as 'sh' and 'th'. In English, one would say, 'thank you' and in Tok Pisin would be 'tenkyu'. Therefore, for someone in Papua New Guinea who speaks fluent Tok Pisin but when speaking to another in English, may say, 'tenkyu' without the 'th' sound.

Thus, in most cases, students and public servants alike in Papua New Guinea seem to make a lot of English errors and often use technical words without even understanding accurately their meanings. Lynch in Turner (1982: 10) suggests that it is advisable to use simple English that can communicate the message across to the listeners or use Tok Pisin or Hiri Motu if certain ideas are difficult to express in English. Similar cases were reported by Holzknecht (1983: 58) among students at the University of Technology in Lae, Papua New Guinea, where students made a lot of spelling mistakes and pronunciation errors and had expression difficulties, mixed vowel and consonant sounds, or had faults in vowels and diphthongs in English.

One of the national government's objectives in enforcing the English-only policy in the education system is to make its people know the scientific language and its associated technical skills of the modern world in order for them to bring about innovation and change to the country. Yes, one would also want to see Papua New Guinea becoming a member of the global community of English speakers for the purpose of international trade, communication and education. To achieve this greater objective, universities and colleges in the country make English an academic tool for scientific and technological research and training is being done. Thus, English tends to become valued by academics and students because it is associated with high status work and subsequent economic benefits.

5.2 Use of English in the Legal Profession in Papua New Guinea
In the legal profession in PNG, the use of English has become rather technical. As Pataki in Thirlwall and Hughes (1989: 19) discovered, most legal concepts are elaborated and deeply rooted in Western culture. There are therefore difficulties in applying them to the customs, values and experiences of the people of Papua New Guinea. The author further argued that those Papua New Guineans who are involved in legal work, such as, lawyers, magistrates, police personnel and the like, seem to have an imperfect understanding of legal concepts in English, particularly technical legal terminology. This difficulty creates more problems for the bulk of Papua New Guineans who are unaware of the law, such as the legal system and their legal rights as citizens of PNG. All statute law in PNG is similarly written in English and therefore, judgements are deliberated on and pronounced in English in the National and Supreme Courts, so that they can not be understood by the majority of Papua New Guineans.

There is however, a flexibility being applied in the Magistrates' Courts at the district and local levels where either vernacular languages or Tok Pisin and other dominant lingua francas are being used. In most Village Courts, and especially where there is a mixture of people from other language groups, Tok Pisin is used, which seems to work well for the people. Generally, English is seen to be causing a major dilemma, especially in relation to its involvement and use. Therefore, legal verdicts or documents in national and supreme courts should be presented in Tok Pisin or any other lingua franca (like Hiri Motu) so that most Papua New Guineans would be clearly aware of the legal issues that they ought to know (see Pataki in Thirlwall and Hughes, 1989: 22).

6. Conclusion

It is seen that English is an official language in which literacy skills are gained through the formal education system in Papua New Guinea. Although it is used to package and disseminate public information so that it has an official monopoly over the other lingua francas, the disadvantages related to it seem to be considerable. Our findings show that the use of English seems to have resulted in most people missing out on vital information, inequalities in the education system, and failure to express PNG cultural values. The adoption of English technical terminologies in the legal system and other public domains cause misunderstandings amongst lawyers, other public servants and the ordinary people of Papua New Guinea. As a result of this, proficiency in English is still seen as a problem, even in educational institutions throughout the country.

Tok Pisin, on the other hand, seems to be playing a dominant role in most social domains, such as: church, homes, parliament, markets, playgrounds, some national and provincial media, village life and so on. It is considered as a social language so that restriction of its use is not evident anywhere except in some schools (Wurm and Mühlhäusler, 1985: 62). In addition, 'code switching' (Hudson, 1990: 57), is more frequent these days with people tending to switch code from English to Tok Pisin and visa-versa. This tendency of code switching can be seen as a result of: people lacking full knowledge of, or confidence in the English language, or being embarrassed when grammatical errors are made in front of others when communicating in English. Sometimes, code switching tends to occur when technical terminologies in English become difficult to explain in English and visa-versa.

Therefore, the use of English in Papua New Guinea and its role so far seems to suggest that, only to a limited extent, does it promote access to public information, and subsequent integral and educational development. This trend will continue if certain drastic actions are not taken by the national government in order to alleviate such linguistic inequalities in Papua New Guinea. The positive view of it as far as greater contributions is concerned, is the fact that, it positively helps to develop a system of education that is similar to the Western world, with its educational and scientific or technological innovations. It would also contribute something positive in international trade, communication and development in PNG.

The possibility making English as one's mother tongue in current Papua New Guinea, even among the English educated elite, appears to be unfavourable and this situation will continue for a long time. This could be the case because of the fact that, the dominant Tok Pisin and the less dominant Hiri Motu and other native languages totalling more than 850, will surely interfere with the efficient use and domestication of the English lingua franca. However, the current trend indicates that English will continue to dominate public life, thus playing a major role in education, politics, law, media, medicine and science and technology in Papua New Guinea.

Notes

1. Most of the literature critique on the topic, 'the role of lingua francas in Papua New Guinea' was summarized from my previous unpublished research work carried out while undertaking my Master of Educational Studies degree at the Adelaide University, South Australia. One also notes that the whole area of 'the role of lingua francas and their contribution to educational development in Papua New Guinea' is currently being dealt with and will be devoted to this subject.
2. I wish to congratulate Dr. Toru Okamura for his inspiration in collating chapters on language issues in Papua New Guinea and elsewhere. This type of collaborative language research and publication is highly appreciated and we need to do more in future.

References

Baldauf, R. B. and Luke, A. (1990) *Language planning and education in Australasia and the South Pacific*, Clevedon, Philadelphia, Multilingual Matters Ltd.

Barbara, D. (2005) *Some facts and figures about the English language, Sao Paulo, Brazil*, Lycee Pasteur, Foreign Language Department.

Education Department (1991) *Education sector review: Executive summary and principle recommendations*, Waigani, PNG, Government House.

Gillian, A. (1989) "Language, communication and power", in Thirlwall, C. and Hughes, P.J. (eds.), *The ethics of development: Language, communication and power*, Port Moresby, University of Papua New Guinea Press.

Hernandez-Chavez, E. (1988) "Language policy and language rights in the United States", in Skutnabb-Kangas, T. and Cummins, J. (eds.), *Minority education: From shame to struggle*, Clevedon/Philadelphia, Multilingual Matters Ltd.

Holzknecht, S. (1983) "Some of the language problems experienced by Papua New Guinea speakers of English", in *TESLA, A magazine for teachers of English as a second language in PNG*, Vol. 2, No. 1. p.58, Waigani, Curriculum Unit.

Hudson, R.A. (1990) *Sociolinguistics*, Cambridge, UK, Cambridge University Press.

Johnson, R.K. (1974) *Language policy in Papua New Guinea*, University of Papua New Guinea, PNG, Teaching Methods and Materials Centre.

Kale, J. (1990) "Language planning and the languages of Papua New Guinea", in Baldauf, R.B. and Luke, A. (eds.), *Language planning and education in Australasia and the South Pacific*, Clevedon, Philadelphia, Multilingual Matters Limited.

Lynch, J. (1982) English and effective communication in the public service, In Turner, M. M. (ed.) *Administration for development*, Waigani, Administrative College of Papua New Guinea.

Ministerial Committee Report (1986) *A philosophy of education for Papua New Guinea*, PNG,

Waigani Government House.

Nekitel, O.M. (1984) *Language planning in Papua New Guinea: A nationalist viewpoint*, Waigani, PNG, University of Papua New Guinea.

Nekitel, O.M. (1989) *Communication studies supplementary readings*, University of Papua New Guinea, Language & Literature Department.

Nekitel. O.M. and Kamene, S. (1991) *Papua New Guinea sociolinguistics: A book of readings*, Waigani, PNG, University of Papua New Guinea.

Parker, N.J. (1986) "Improvement of spoken English of professional Papua New Guineans", in *TESLA, A magazine for teachers of English as a second language in Papua New Guinea*, Vol. iv. No.3, p.42, Waigani, Curriculum Unit.

Pataki, L.S. "Issues in the use of legal language in Papua New Guinea", in Thirlwall, C. and Hughes, P.J. (eds.) *The ethics of development: Language, communication and power*, Port Moresby, University of Papua New Guinea Press.

Piau, J. Lynch, J. and Crowley, T. (1992) *Communication and language: Reader*, Waigani, PNG, University of Papua New Guinea.

Post-Courier, Wednesday May 10, 1995:10.

Post-Courier, Thursday June 28, 1995:10.

Roebuck, D. (1989) "Law and language: The ethics of ignorance", in Thirlwall, C. and Hughes, P.J. (eds.), *The ethics of development: Language, communication and power*, Port Moresby, University of Papua New Guinea Press.

Siegruhn, A. (1994) *Editorial: EWE to reconstruction and development*, Vol. 9, No.3, cover page, Salt River, South Africa.

Skutnabb-Kangas, T. and Cummins, J. (1988) *Minority education: From shame to struggle*, Clevedon/Philadelphia, Multilingual Matters Ltd.

Smolicz, J.J. (1979) *Education and culture in a plural society*, Canberra, Curriculum Development Centre.

Smolicz, J.J. (1992) *Australian diversity, language – A bridge or a barrier?*, University of Adelaide, Centre for Intercultural Studies and Multilingual Education.

Thirlwall, C. and Hughes, P.J. (1989) *The ethics of development: Language, communication and power*, Port Moresby, University of Papua New Guinea Press.

Times of Papua New Guinea, Tuesday February 23, 1995:8.

Turner, M. M. (1982) *Administration for development*, Waigani, Administrative College of Papua New Guinea.

Wurm, S.A. and Mühlhäusler, P. (1985) *Handbook of Tok Pisin (New Guinea Pidgin)*, Pacific Linguistic Series, C-No. 7D; Department of Linguistics Research School of Pacific Studies, Canberra, Australian National University.

Znaniecki, F. (1982) "The Polish memoir sociology. Origins – dilemmas – hopes" in Adamski, W.W.et. al, (eds.), *Sisyphus, sociological studies*, Warsaw, PWN – Polish Scientific Publishers.

On the Degree of Contact Language Stabilization: A Contrastive Study of Tok Pisin and Nauruan Pidgin

Toru Okamura
Tezukayama Gakuin University, Japan

1. Introduction

The aim of this paper is to discuss the rules, relations and systems of contact languages affecting decline and endangering their existence, with special reference to Tok Pisin and Nauruan Pidgin. I will advance a cline theory to explain the degree of contact language stabilization. Tok Pisin is one of the most stable contact languages, and Nauruan Pidgin is positioned in the middle of a continuum.

Although many studies have been made on language decline, little is known about their degree of stability. Language decline studies often fail to grasp the relation between the factors leading to decline. Namely, few linguists agree on how to explain the phenomenon. The paper enumerates some components and relates them to contact languages on continents and islands. The position of Tok Pisin and Nauruan Pidgin in a continuum for the degree of stabilization can be demonstrated by showing contrastive and sociolinguistic approaches historically and structurally with other pidgins and creoles. Now we shall survey the linguistic situations in Papua New Guinea and Nauru.

The socio-historical background of Tok Pisin is related to sugarcane in Western Samoa and Queensland. The vocabulary layers of Tok Pisin are basically based on English and Tolai, one of the Austronesian languages in Melanesia, except some words from European languages like German. This means the impact of Tolai tribes on the formation of Tok Pisin was enormous. Firstly, I give an example to illustrate phonetic correspondence between Tok Pisin and Tolai. For instance, Tok Pisin '*tumbuna*' (ancestors) corresponds to *tubuna* in Tolai. Similarly, *tarangu* (miserable) to *taragu*, and *kindam* (a crayfish) to *kidama*. The nasal sound before the voiced stop is lost in this pattern.

Also, correspondence can be seen in the area of open to closed syllables, though not all. *Kapiak* (*breadfruit tree and fruit* from Mihalic 1971: 106) corresponds to *kapiaka* in Tolai. Similarly, *bulit* (*sticky sap of certain trees, especially the breadfruit* from Mihalic 1971: 78) becomes *bulita*, and *kindam* for *kidama*.

In Tok Pisin, there are four varieties. Each variety plays an important role in their community. Tok Pisin is a national language as well as lingua franca between tribes in Papua New Guinea. It is the language of government, education, business, church and mass media. For most people it is the language for job-seeking. Hence, Tok Pisin is used in all domains and activities. Furthermore, the sociolinguistic situation is becoming increasingly complicated.

There are many structural similarities as well. Let us start with the predicate marker which is widely used in Melanesian languages. The predicate marker in Tolai occurs when the subject is a third person singular pronoun or noun phrase subject. Then the predicate co-occurs with only predicate adjectives, not predicate nouns.

(1) Dat   boinaka.
    3pl   fine
    'They are fine.'
(2) Kau-gu   pi   vakir   i   boina.
    land-of   my   not   PM   good
    'My land is not good.'

On the other hand, the predicate marker does not relate to the nature of the verb in Tok Pisin. It occurs when the subject is the third person singular/plural or noun phrase subject. In addition, it occurs when the subject is a first person pronoun. Generally, the frequency of predicate markers in Tok Pisin is much greater than in Tolai.

(3) Em   i   lapun.
    3sg   PM   old
    'He is old.'
(4) Em   i   orait.
    3sg   PM   fine
    'He is fine.'
(5) Papamama   bilong yu   i   orait?
    parents   of   you   PM   fine
    'Are your parents fine?'
(6) Ol   i   pren   bilong mi.
    3pl   PM   friend of   me
    'They are my friends.'

Tolai and Tok Pisin do not correspond precisely in the nature of predicate marker; however the core nature of the predicate marker is basically the same. Several other examples show similarity such as transitivity and past tense marker.

Okamura (1990: 168) explored in detail the occurrence of predicate markers by using stories and newspapers written in Tok Pisin. It showed the occurrence of predicate markers is highly consistent in formal style, but inconsistent in informal style. For example, in *Wantok Niuspepa* the percentage of predicate markers is high, but in the cartoon column in the paper the ellipsis of the predicate marker is common.

Romaine (1993: 251) examined the relation between TMA markers and predicate marker in Tok Pisin. She noticed the loss of the predicate marker, especially among younger urban speakers.

Nauru is the smallest nation republic in the world (21 square kilometres). It is situated just south of the equator near Ocean Island and has a tropical climate. Captain John Fearn was the first European to sight Nauru in 1798. Germany administered Nauru until 1914. Japan occupied Nauru in 1942 and stayed three years. The Australian currency is used. Today Nauru is governed by the Nauruan Parliament. Three main languages are spoken on the island: Nauruan, English and

Nauruan Pidgin. The Nauruans are Christian and education is compulsory from six to 16. Because of its phosphates, its GDP is the highest in the Pacific islands, but phosphate exports are decreasing. Migrant workers contribute to developing Nauruan society.

Many different nationalities in Nauru are shown in the 1992 census (Demmke et. al, 1999) because of the government's policy. It shows 69% of Nauru's population was made up of indigenous Nauruans; almost 24% were from Kiribati and Tuvalu and 6 per cent were from China and the Philippines.

In 1907, Chinese labourers were first imported in order to dig phosphate. After that each year approximately 1,000 Chinese labourers worked on the island. The contracts were for three years, but they could renew their contracts. Their Pidgin English was brought to the island to communicate with Nauruan people in the stores, restaurants and workshops in phosphate mining. Over the years, it developed and changed and is still spoken today—for example:

(7)
NS: Wat   abaut   the   kastama,   Mista   Chan?
    what   about   DET   customer   mr   Chan
    'How about the customer, Mr Chan?'
CS: Yes,   it's   gud.
    yes   it's   good
    'Yes, it's good.'
NS: Yu   gat   pipul   kam?
    2sg   get   people   come
    'Do you have many people to come (to the restaurant)?'
CS: We   get   kastama   everi   dei.
    1pl   get   customer   every   day
    'We get many customers every day.'
NS: Many   kastama   ya?
    many   customer   yeh
    'Many customers?'

CS:	Yes,	faiv	o	siks.
	yes	five	or	six

'Yes, five or six.'

NS:	Yu	get	mani.
	2sg	get	many

'Can you get money?'

(NS = Nauruan Speaker, CS = Chinese Speaker)　　(Okamura 2003: 25)

This Pidgin is called Nauruan Pidgin by the author, though it is based on Chinese Coast Pidgin. Since then, this pidgin has been influenced by several Pacific Pidgin Englishes and altered at some linguistic levels.

The author asked Chinese speakers about the use of language in several locations in the districts Denigomodu, Aiwo, Boe, Yaren, Meneng and Nibok on the island in 1998. The questionnaire was prepared and the author visited restaurants and stores in many districts of the nation. The data come from 47 Chinese speakers. Almost half were men. Most residents were from Canton (44), two from Hong Kong and one from Taiwan. All were Cantonese speakers. Twenty-two work in stores, 14 in restaurants, one in the Nauru Phosphate Company, one in dry cleaning. Eleven speakers graduated from primary school, 12 from secondary, one from senior high school, one from university and one was uneducated. Twenty-one were in their twenties, 11 in their 30s, three in their 40s, two were teenagers. The results are outlined below:

(1) They had a Cantonese background.
(2) They worked in commercial contexts like restaurants and stores.
(3) They spoke Cantonese and Pidgin English.
(4) They had resided in Nauru less than five years.

(Okamura 2003: 29)

Okamura (1998: 35) collected the following opinions of each other:

[Nauruan attitudes]: Chinese just work and work for the money on the island. That's all. Their sense of values differs from ours. We (Nauruans) are superior to the Chinese in social class. What is really annoying for us is that we have to use Pidgin, not English when they do not understand what we say.

[Chinese attitudes]: Nauruans do not work at all. Also they do not go to school to study. We have trouble because they sometimes do not pay in our restaurants and stores.

Many Chinese people wish to buy Nauruan passports in order to do their business in other parts of the world successfully. Relevant to this point is Okamura's above collection. Chinese everyday life on the island used to be very insecure for historical reasons. However, their importance in roles and positions in the community is increasing more and more. Because of the decline of phosphates, the economic situation in Nauru is bad, so they have to construct new industries such as tourism and fisheries. The Nauru government seems to recognize that not only Nauruan people but also other immigrants are needed to develop the nation. The Chinese people might be encouraged and allowed to do their own business if the government improves its relationships with other Asia-Pacific countries.

2. Features of Tok Pisin and Nauruan Pidgin

Before turning to a closer examination of language decline, a few remarks should be made concerning language structure in Tok Pisin and Nauruan Pidgin. Siegel (1990) examines features of Nauruan Pidgin compared to those of Chinese PE (Pidgin English) and Pacific PE. He looked at characteristics of Chinese PE in Nauruan Pidgin not found in Pacific PE. He also looked at distinctive Pacific PE features; shared features and distinguishing features of Chinese PE and Pacific PE respectively. His views on the features have much in common with those of this author (1998). However, there are some further linguistic phenomena that we must not ignore. And Siegel did not touch upon the features of Nauruan people.

The following table outlines the features of Nauruan Pidgin and Tok Pisin

(TP = Tok Pisin, NP1 = Pidgin English by Nauruans, NP2 = Pidgin spoken by Chinese). The data was tape-recorded for three hours from three informants on the island in 1998.

Abbreviations:

Incl. = inclusive/excl. = exclusive/N = noun/Pro = pronoun/1sg = first person singular subject/1pl = first person plural subject/PM = predicate marker/2sg = second person singular subject/3pl = third person plural subject/3sg = third person singular subject/P = preposition/TAG = tag question

Table 1. Features of Tok Pisin and Nauruan Pidgin

	TP	NP1	NP2
1. Distinction between incl./excl.	+	−	−
2. N+bilong+Pro.	+	−	−
3. Pronoun copying	+	+	+
4. Predicate marker *i*	+	−	−
5. Past tense marker *bin*	+	−	−
6. Future tense marker *bai*	+	−	+
7. Progressive aspect *i stap*	+	−	−
8. Past perfect tense marker *pinis*	+	−	−
9. Existential construction marker *i gat*	+	−	−
10. Transitive marker *–im*	+	−	−
11. Habitual action marker *save*	+	−	+
12. Preposition *long*	+	+	+
13. Bimorphemic question words	+	−	−
14. Auxiliary *ken*	+	+	+
15. Adjectival suffix *–pela*	+	+ (?)	+
16. Negative marker *no*	+	+	+
17. Quantitative *olgeta*	+	−	+
18. Distinction between singular/plural	+	−	−
19. Suffixes showing numbers and pronouns *–pela*	+	− (?)	−
20. Tag question *raka*	+	−	−
21. Vowel addition	−	+	+
22. Numeral classifier *piecee*	−	+	+

Source: Okamura (2003: 57)

What table 1 makes clear at once is that the general point is that Nauruan Pidgin today is largely based on China Coast Pidgin. Features of China Coast Pidgin are shown in Siegel (1990). Nauruan Pidgin is a living language. The development process can be schematized as follows:

Nauruan Pidgin < China Coast Pidgin
[or A < B (A is derived from B)]

There is considerable validity to this concept, though it should not be pushed too far. Pidgin English spoken by Nauruans is similar to that of Pidgin spoken by Chinese on the island. Even if there are some disagreements between NP1 and NP2, this does not affect the validity of the above schema.

We shall discuss it in detail. First, the distinction of incl./excl. is very important as a grammatical device that Austronesian languages distinguish. For instance, it can be seen in Tok Pisin. This example from Franklin 1968 (Okamura 1990: 173) makes it clear that it relates to substratum theory (*Dat a oro ra pusi.* 'We will call the cat.' *Amital a oro.* 'We will call out (for).') . However, the trace cannot be seen in Pidgin spoken by the Chinese and Nauruans. There is a distinction, but it is not lexicalized.

(8) TP: Yumi   go   long   skul.
        1pl   go   to   school
        'You and I go to school.'
        Mipela   i   go   long   skul.
        1pl   PM   go   to   school
        'He and I go to school.'
   NP1: Mi   yu   go   skul.
        1sg   2sg   go   school
        'You and I go to school.'
        Ada   boi   an   mi   go   skul.
        other   boy(3sg) and   1sg   go   school
        'He and I go to school.'
   NP2: Blong   mi   blong   yu   go   skul.
        of   me   of   you   go   school
        'You and I go to school.'
        Blong   mi   blong   ada   men   go   skul.
        of   me   of   other   men   go   school
        'He and I go to school.'

(Okamura 2003: 31)

In Pacific Pidgin English, there is a morphological distinction in the first person plural pronoun not seen in Pidgin on the island. It is pointed out that lack of solidarity does not produce the grammatical device, but the problem is how we consider the solidarity. Rather, it is likely that it is based on substratum influence. The *blong* used by the Chinese tend to drop out in utterances. Thus, Pidgin spoken by Nauruans could plausibly be derived from the Pidgin of the Chinese.

Secondly, transitivity can be expressed by the suffix *–im* in Tok Pisin. Again it is clear that the nature of transitivity in Tok Pisin corresponds to that of Tolai (*Iau iliba*. 'I will gather.' *Iau ilibe ra purpur*. 'I am gathering the flowers.' From Flanklin 1968 in Okamura 1990: 173). However, in Pidgin on the island, it is not common.

(9) TP: Mi   wasim   T-shat   bilong   mi.
         1sg   wash   T-shirt of   me
         'I wash my T-shirts.'
         Mi   kisim   shawa.
         1sg   take   shower
         'I take a shower.'

NP1:   Mi   was   mi   T-shat.
         1sg   wash   my   T-shirt
         'I wash my T-shirts.'
         Mi   tek   shawa.
         1sg   take   shower
         'I take a shower.'

NP2:   Mi   wasi   blong   mi   T-shat.
         1sg   wash   of   me   T-shirt
         'I wash my T-shirts.'
         Mi   laigi   sawa.
         1sg   like   shower
         'I take a shower.'

(Okamura 2003: 32)

The *wasi* is not a contracted form of *wasim*, but vowel addition as shown later. The Nauru language has a transitive suffix, but this form is not incorporated into Pidgin.

Thirdly, existential sentences can be shown by using *gat* in many pidgins and creoles. Pidgin on the island is no exception. The use of *gat* is optional in the Pidgin used by the Chinese and Nauruans, but in Pacific Pidgin, it is a must. In this respect, the three pidgins are not the same in nature, but it would be better to think that Nauruan Pidgin is similar to that of Pacific Pidgin in that one common lexical item can be used in two different linguistic environments.

(10) TP: Mi   gat   tupela   pikinini.
     1sg   get   two   child
     'I have only two children.'
     I   gat   tupela   pikinini long   hotel.
     there is   two   child   in   hotel
     'There are two children in the hotel.'
   NP1: Mi   onli   tu   gadudu.
        1sg   only   two   child
        'I have only two children.'
        Tu   gadudu   in   the   otel.
        two   child   in   the   hotel
        'There are two children in the hotel.'
   NP2: Blong   mi   tu   piecee   gadudu.
        of   me   two   NUM   child
        'I have only two children.'
        Tu   gadudu   stap   otel.
        two   child   stay   hotel
        'There are two children in the hotel.'

(Okamura 2003: 32)

At the same time Nauruan Pidgin tends to be less used in social functions because of the decline of the Chinese population and because of its co-existence with Pacific Pidgin. Pidginization shows some distinguishing features of Chinese Pidgin English. For instance, Siegel (1990: 168) says that *by and by* (future tense marker) is one of 'the three shared features which are not found in the data and which most likely do not occur in Nauruan Pidgin'. However, the future tense marker was recognized by the author as follows:

(11) NS: Bambai yu fren kam?
FTM you friend come
'Are your friends coming?'
CS: Everidei kam see mi.
everyday come see me
'They are coming everyday.'

(Okamura 2003: 33)

Local people may show some individual variation but this trend indicates mixing with Pacific Pidgin English. In Nauru, the existence of Solomon islanders including Gilbertese is important in that they bring Pacific Pidgin to the island. This facilitates mixing with Pacific Pidgin in the context of Chinese stores and restaurants where the Pacific Islanders are employed. In addition to this, technical workers come to the Island from the Solomon Islands every year.

Tense and aspect markers in Pidgin on the island are usually expressed by adverbial phrases.

(12) TP: Asde em i go long Tarawa, a?
yesterday 3sg PM go P Tarawa TAG
'Yesterday she went to Tarawa, didn't she?'
Bai em i stap long wanpela wik.
FTM she PM stay for one week
'She will stay here for one week.'
Em i pilai tennis i stap.

		3sg	PM	play	tennis	PM	stay

'She is playing tennis now.'

NP1:   Shi   go   Tarawa yesterdei,   is   shi?
        3sg   go   Tarawa yesterday   TAG

'Yesterday she went to Tarawa, didn't she?'

        Shi   stei   hia   wan   wik.
        3sg   stay   here   one   week

'She will stay here for one week.'

        Nau   shi   plei   tenis.
        now   3sg   play   tennis

'She is playing tennis now.'

        Shi   finis   plei   tenis.
        3sg   finish   play   tennis

'She has just finished playing tennis.'

NP2:   Ada   men   go   Tarawa.
        other   men   go   Tarawa

'He went to Tarawa.' or 'He is going to Tarawa.'

        Ada   gal   stap   wan   wik.
        other   girl   stay   one   week

'She will stay here for one week.'

(Okamura 2003: 33)

The past tense marker *bin* is one of the most frequently used in Pidgins and Creoles in the world. In Tok Pisin, *bin* is often used and its form differs from that of its Tolai equivalent *ga*, but its grammatical function is almost the same (*A bul i ga tangi*. 'A baby cried.' from Franklin in Okamura 1990: 176). However, both Siegel (1990) and the author were unable to find evidence for this marker in the data. I personally expect that the item will be stabilized like *bambai* (or *bai*) and *i* if contact between Pacific Islanders and local people increases.

I agree with Siegel in thinking that koineization has begun in Nauruan Pidgin. But it was in the earlier stages that it began, and now mixing with Pacific

Pidgin is going on. In Nauru, the existence of Solomon Islanders is important in that they bring Solomon Pidgin to the island. This facilitates mixing with Pacific Pidgin in the context of Chinese stores and restaurants where the Solomon Islanders are employed. In addition to this, technical workers come to the island from the Solomon Islands every year.

Furthermore, the predicate marker and transitive marker can be seen in some parts of conversations. Many scholars believe that the nature of predicate marker in Tok Pisin is similar to that of Austronesian (Tolai: *Keake i boinaka* 'Sun is nice.'). It will be clear from these examples that language mixing is going on.

(13) TP: Em   i   gat   bikpela   watch.
          3sg   PM   get   big   watch
         'He has a big watch.'
          Ol   i   naispela.
          3pl   PM   nice
         'They are good-looking.'

 NP1:   Hi   gat   big (fela)   watch.
         3sg   get   big   watch
        'He has a big watch.'
         Dei   planti   gud.
         3pl   plenty   good
        'They are good-looking.'

 NP2:   Ada   men   i   gat   watch.
         other men   PM   get   watch
        'He has a big watch.'
         Dei   planti   gud.
         3pl   plenty   good
        'They are good-looking.'

(Okamura 2003: 35)

Regardless of the nature of the verb, the Tok Pisin predicate marker occurs with any pronoun except first and second singular person pronouns. But in the Pidgin spoken by the Chinese and Nauruans it is uncommon; however it would be better for us to think that language mixing with Pacific Pidgin is going on. The population of Pacific from Islanders 1922 to 1966 was small compared with that of today, as mentioned earlier. Thus, the influence from Pacific Pidgin English is much greater than in the past.

Siegel (1990) pointed out that in Nauruan Pidgin final vowels are added onto some words of English origin. And in some cases, they are optionally used. [i] is most frequently used, then [o] and [u]. The following data reached the author from informants who read vocabulary lists which include 200 words. The first point to notice is that Nauruans use this form more often than the Chinese. More noteworthy is Nauruan use of *killuu* for kill, on the other hand Chinese do not say it in such a way (the origin of *sadui* is unknown yet it is used by the Chinese).

In Nauruan phonology, such linguistic phenomena cannot be seen. These might be hypercorrective errors, where the speaker actually mispronounces a form in trying to communicate and imitate the form in commercial contexts. The phenomenon usually occurs when he/she tries to pronounce a stigmatized form. There may be some objections to this analysis, but the phenomenon admits of no other explanation.

(14) Examples of Vowel Addition + Vowel Lengthening
[Cantonese speaker]:

laikee 'like'	auntee 'aunt'
mouthee 'mouth'	housee 'house'
citee 'city'	plantee 'plenty'
yesuu 'church'	geluu 'girl'
faifuu 'five'	uncluu 'uncle'
hospituu 'hospital'	

[Nauruan speaker]:
changee 'change'	risee 'rise'
watchee 'watch'	pushee 'push'
cutee 'cut'	clothee 'cloth'
dancee 'dance'	touchee 'touch'
auntee 'aunt'	citee 'city'
facee 'face'	churchee 'church'
plantee 'plenty'	smiluu 'smile'
killuu 'kill'	uncluu 'uncle'
wifuu 'wife'	geluu 'girl'

[Tok Pisin speaker]:
laik 'like'	ant 'aunt'
siti 'city'	plenti 'plenty'

(Okamura 2003: 36)

There is one other important characteristic of Nauruan Pidgin, the numerical classifier *piecee*. Siegel (1990) classified it as a distinctive Chinese Pidgin English feature. I agree with Siegel in thinking that the element is distinctively Chinese. According to Todd (1984: 260), this is very commonly used and 'derived from a piece or bale of calico, which is the staple import of British manufactured goods.' Furthermore the tendency to use 'piecee' as an adjectival marker is similar to that of the use of -pela in Tok Pisin (p.259). As Todd (1984: 260) supposes, the trader had to try to impress upon the Chinese buyer that his belongings, for example shirtings are 'number one'.

I do not object to the above, however, it is also considered that the British traders simplified their speech like 'one piece' or 'two pieces' in communicating with the Chinese, and the Chinese people might have added a vowel to the end like 'piecee' as I mentioned. Then it spread all over the coastal area of China and was brought to Nauru. The usage of 'piecee' itself is similar to that of Chinese, or word order 'numeral+numeral marker+noun'. But the form of the numeral marker in Chinese varies with the variety of noun. However, we must not forget that –pela in Tok Pisin has some grammatical functions. Thus it does not correspond to that of the usage of Tok Pisin. Again the following example shows Pidgin spoken by Nauruans is similar to that of the Chinese.

(15) CS: Mi   (gat)   faiv (piecee)   gadudu.
        1sg   get   five   child
        'I have got five children.'
   NS: Mi   gat   faiv   piecee   gadudu.
        1sg   get   five   NUM   child
        'I have got five children.'
   TP: Mi   gat   faipela   pikinini.
        1sg   get   five   child
        'I have got five children.'

                                                                     (Okamura 2003: 38)

Siegel (1990: 171-172) found some unique lexical features in Nauru Pidgin English. There were, however, only two words from Nauruan, *gadudu* 'child' and *kumo* 'pig'. Okamura (2003: 38) also pointed out that these were the only two words recognized by the author from the tape-recording.

(16) CS: Hia   wat   yu   kaikai?
        here   what   2sg   eat
        'What would you like to have here?'
   NS: Kumo   rais.
        pig   rice
        'Rice with pork.'

Gadudu and *kumo* are most frequently used in Pidgin English in Nauru. And it is true that we could only recognize those two words in Pidgin English in Nauru. A Nauruan-based pidgin has not occurred so far and probably will not develop in the future. This should be said with some emphasis. There are a few possible answers for this. For one thing the importance of the Nauruan's language attitude to Nauruan Pidgin cannot be overemphasized. The Pidgin has been stigmatized by Nauruans with concepts like 'Chinese', 'working class', 'lacking Nauru character'. Such attitudes resulted from the reduction of Nauruans' opportunities to come into contact with the Chinese. This is not to say that Nauruan people do not try to use Pidgin. Generally speaking, the use of vocabulary is important to keep one's identity. Nauruans tend to think that Pidgin belongs to the Chinese, thus they do not want to use their speech in a pidginized context.

Moreover, Nauruans and Chinese did not mix freely in the past. Originally Chinese came into contact with Pacific Islanders and other Asians in the context of phosphate mining. This facilitated the mixing of Nauruan Pidgin with Pacific Pidgin as mentioned above.

A final point is that European lands such as Britain, Germany and Australia have governed the island, so the dominance of European languages still continues. A hierarchy from English which enjoys prestige, to Pidgin which has low status, has formed in the community. It is likely that this hierarchy prevented Nauruan words from entering Pidgin. One certainty is that Nauruan Pidgin has been mixing with Pacific Pidgin.

One can safely state that Nauruan Pidgin is based on China Coast Pidgin. The origin of Pacific Pidgin remains a matter for debate. For instance, Wurm (in Mühlhäusler 1985) and Hancock (1971: 523) believe the influence of Chinese Pidgin has been enormous on the development of Pacific Pidgin English. On the other hand, Hall (1961) and Clark (1980) entirely disagree with this Chinese origin. The fuller study of the origin of Nauruan Pidgin lies outside the scope of this paper and I will not dwell on the matter. It seems reasonable to suppose that the Nauruan Pidgin is derived from Chinese Pidgin, as can be seen earlier from the discussion of the structure of Nauruan Pidgin.

It should be concluded, from what has been said above, that language mixing is still going on. Features of Pacific Pidgin in Nauruan Pidgin can be explained by the influx of Pacific Islanders like Solomon Islanders including Gilbertese at

Chinese stores and restaurants.

3. Factors affecting contact language stability

Let us return to our main subject. I want to show that both geographical and socio-political factors influence a speaker's perception of the contact language. I will use the term "geographical factors" to refer to whether or not the contact language is spoken on continents or islands, and how much the super-stratum language affects the contact language in a community.

The term "socio-political factors" can be defined as the changed socio-political distance between host and immigrant societies. It includes political factors, living environment, social factors, institutional factors and mass media. I will use the term "socio-political factors" to refer to the degree of stability. To put it more concretely, "political factors" indicate whether the contact language is or is not a national (or official) language, and stable or not. The "living environment" means the living space is not isolated, but tends to spread.

"Social factors" refer to a speaker's low social class while the numbers in a speech community are decreasing. "Institutional factors" imply the contact language is not adopted in education and speakers seldom find ways to advance in a community. "Mass media" reveal the contact language is not used for television, radio and newspapers, so is restricted to homes and some non-official domains. I should make it clear what I intend by these expressions. The point I want to make is that there is a cline for the factors. We miss the point if we regard all factors as having the same import.

Political factors are considered some of the most influential in a cline. That goes to the very core of the problem. For example, in Australia, the Commonwealth government legislated the deportation of all immigrant Melanesians in 1901. This facilitated a gradual but total change from Kanaka English to English. On the other hand, institutional factors including mass media are ambivalent in a cline. At the beginning of the 20th century, the New South Wales government tried to prohibit the use of Norfolk in the school system on

Norfolk Island, however the language is not endangered because Pitcairn-descent Norfolk Islanders heightened their solidarity by using Norfolk among themselves. Nauruan Pidgin is not used for radio, television and newspapers in Nauru, but it is still alive.

These linguistic and historical facts show those factors that have little weakening effect on contact languages. It would be untrue to say that the factor "mass media" is equivalent to that of political ones in degree. The factor is weaker than people's living environment. If group solidarity collapses, the maintenance of the language weakens. Social discrimination often makes speakers cling more closely to each other, so that the language does not die out among the younger generation.

Cline

Political factors > Living environment > Social factors > Institutional factors > Mass media

The above cline makes it possible to interpret language decline. Thus geographical as well as socio-political factors influence the speaker's identity (In other words, "psychological factors" defines how far a person tries to keep his or her mother tongue or contact language). In the following two sections I shall be examining some contact languages spoken on continents and islands.

3.1 Relations with contact languages on continents

Two points seem to be helpful in attempting to sketch out contact language stability. We will begin by considering features of contact languages on continents. What are their components? First, geographical pressure is enormous. Secondly, socio-political pressure is enormous, thus the speaker's cultural self-identity and desire to try to keep his or her mother tongue or contact language is weak. Thirdly, the contact language is easy to spread because the common code system is easily produced.

Nothing will illustrate political factors better than Kanaka English. Kanaka

English was widely spoken throughout Queensland from the late 19th century to the early 20th century. The White Australia Policy forced Kanakas back home until 1906. Between 1,600 and 2,500 Kanakas remained in Australia. The numbers of speakers may or may not have had a bearing on successful language maintenance. The settlement shift from sugar town communities to non-sugar towns caused language decline. Society on the plantations altered from Kanaka to European domination. This led to the loss of vertical (master-servant) communication in restricted labour contexts. The change might have decreased the opportunities for promoting solidarity among them. In addition, the loss of identity would have been important in the shift. Kanakas made no effort to promote internal solidarity among themselves. Their language probably also declined because they lost ties with their homeland and had to survive under different circumstances. Such insecurity and a feeling of loss caused sporadic identity crisis.

Chinese Pidgin English (Australia) and China Coast Pidgin (China) are other notable examples.

Fig.2 Features of contact languages on continents

	KE	CPA	CPC	K	NP	CP
1	+	+	+	−	−	−
2	+	+	+	+?	−	−
3	+	+	+	−	−	−
4	+	+	+	−	−	−

1   geographical pressure is enormous
2   socio-political pressure is enormous
3   speaker's insistence on keeping his or her mother tongue or contact language is low
4   contact language spreads easily because the common code system other than contact languages is likely to be produced

KE: Kanaka English, CPA: Chinese Pidgin in Australia, CPC: Chinese Pidgin in

China, K: Kriol, NP: Nigerian Pidgin English, CP: Cameroon Pidgin English

+ denotes the contact language fills its component, whereas – shows it does not fill the element. ? suggests we cannot say for certain whether or not it is + or -.

I shall outline here how we could judge + or – in the diagram. The judgement is mainly based on previous descriptions and my fieldwork in the past. Nigerian and Cameroon Pidgin English are not subject to the above rule. This is not to deny that my hypothesis is valid. They have almost the same linguistic environment as on islands, keeping political power, autonomy and sociolinguistic diversity in that the language is in part of a structural and functional hierarchy.

Kriol (Australia) is partially subject to the rule. This means Kriol is positioned in the middle of a continuum. In some sense, the socio-political pressure of Kriol is enormous in that Aboriginal people were gathered in reserves, and also experienced the Second World War. But these facts promoted solidarity among them. Thus Kriol stabilized in the Northern Territory. We may consider the subject under the following heading: (1) socio-political pressure to promote solidarity; (2) socio-political pressure not to promote solidarity.

3.2 Relations with contact languages on islands

The question to consider next is relations with contact languages on islands. What are its components? First, geographical pressure is low. Secondly, socio-political pressure is low, so the speaker's desire to keep his or her mother tongue or contact language is enormous. Thirdly, the contact language is likely to be preserved because a common code system other than contact languages is lacking.

Tok Pisin is an example satisfying its components. Geographically, Papua New Guinea is the nearest nation to Australia, however it is a multi-tribal nation. Thus English influences the society extremely little because New Guinean society keeps its sociolinguistic diversity: 700 local vernaculars and lingua francas such as Tok Pisin and Hiri Motu are spoken. Thus geographical pressure is low. Tok Pisin had official recognition in the national Constitution and in Parliament. This political situation contributed to stabilizing Tok Pisin in various domains among

Papua New Guineans. That Tok Pisin gained some official status is important to consider its stability. Tok Pisin speakers are proud of using it today. There are several other examples. Pijin (Solomon Islands) and Bislama (Vanuatu) belong to the same class.

Fig.3 Features of contact languages on islands

	P	TP	SP	Bi	NP	N	Br	MP
1	+	+	+	+	+	+?	+??	-
2	+	+	+	+	+	+?	+??	-
3	+	+	+	+	+?	+?	+	-
4	+	+	+	+	+	+?	+	-

1 geographical pressure is low
2 socio-political pressure is low
3 speakers try hard to keep his or her mother tongue (or contact language)
4 contact language is likely to be preserved because a common code system other than contact languages is lacking
P: Pitcairnese, TP: Tok Pisin, SP: Solomon Pijin, Bi: Bislama, NP: Nauruan Pidgin, N: Norfolk, Br: Broken, MP: Maori Pidgin

Maori Pidgin is not subject to the rule above. It was spoken on islands yet disappeared. The rule does not apply to this case, however, again this is not to deny that my hypothesis is valid. It can be explained by the fact that in Maori Pidgin demographically Westerners are dominant, and the political power or autonomy is weak so that it lacks sociolinguistic diversity. It is therefore not in a strong structural or functional position in the cline hierarchy.

Nauruan Pidgin, Norfolk and Broken are in the middle of a continuum. Whether the speakers of Nauruan Pidgin are proud of using it is an important and difficult question because there is only limited information. Underwood's study (1988) may contribute to the understanding of accent and identity. He examined the relation between identification index and /ai/ occurrences in Texas English. The same may be said of Nauruan Pidgin. Nauruan Pidgin's vocabulary is characterized by the numerical marker *piecee*. We could examine the occurrence of *piecee* in conversations. Then we could score each informant. In addition, some questions measuring solidarity as a speaker of Nauruan Pidgin are prepared. Finally, the relation between them can be analysed. It is too involved a subject to be treated here in detail.

Norfolk Island has been an Australian territory since 1914 and islanders are much influenced by English. But they keep a different identity because one third of the population is of Pitcairn descent, i.e., of Polynesian elements, though young Norfolk speakers do not have a strong solidarity today. About one third of the population is of Australian descent. The Islanders have many opportunities for contact with mainlanders because of tourism and the economy. Some Norfolk Islanders support independence for Norfolk Island, others do not. This situation makes the language in a continuum.

The Torres Strait is also part of Australia. Geographically, it is close to the mainland and takes in much English influence. Some parents try to migrate to the mainland to make their children learn English. However the number of Islanders is great so that they can sustain sociolinguistic diversity: local languages, Creole and English. Bilingual education is advanced and going on even today. We are now able to see that contact languages spoken on islands differ from that of continents. We have considered some factors for declining contact languages both on continents and islands. Let us demonstrate my position in the next section more fully.

4. Demonstrations

In the preceding section I pointed out the difference between continents and islands. Let us now look at the phenomenon in detail from a different angle. The purpose of this section is to demonstrate what I advanced in the previous sections. Haarman (1985) shows a linguistic ecology model with special reference to political and psychological factors. Most people accept what Haarman pointed out.

What is not so widely understood, however, is how to explain the degree of stability by scoring each contact language. This point deserves explicit emphasis. I have developed the idea a little further by scoring each contact language. ○ means zero point, × means one point.

Fig.4 Degree of contact language stability

Conditions	NP	KE	TP
Ethno-political factors			
• special right to keep the speech community is not added	○	○	×
• language X is national (or official) language	○	○	×
• language X has no official status	○	○	×
• language X is not adopted in education	○	○	×
• opportunities for social advancement among members of the speech community is restricted	○	○	×

Using Haarman's theory, each contact language was scored as follows:

27 points	23~25	14~15	5~9
Tok Pisin	Broken	**Nauruan Pidgin**	Maori Pidgin
Pijin	Pitcairnese		Kanaka English
Bislama	Norfolk		

Judging from the above, most of us would agree that the results support what I advanced in the previous section as our results agree with those obtained by the preceding section, showing that Tok Pisin is one of the most stable languages, and Maori Pidgin unstable. We should notice that both Maori Pidgin and Kanaka English scores are equivalent to the relation of the current linguistic situation because Kanaka English is no longer spoken but it got 5 ~ 9 points. Such work makes it possible to interpret the position of Nauruan Pidgin. It is positioned in the middle of a continuum. In other words, the alternative of stable or unstable does not give a good account of the position of Nauruan Pidgin. If we look at the factors by scoring them objectively, we can observe contact languages located in between in the continuum like this. Such thinking is reflected in languages outside Oceania in many ways.

One can cite many languages in the same way which seem to support this. Let us verify contact languages outside Oceania. First we will examine China Coast Pidgin, Krio and Gullah. They have got 15, 22 and 11 points respectively.

There is no need to go into detail about Krio and Gullah. As far as China Coast Pidgin is concerned, the result contradicts what we examined in that it is no longer spoken in China, however it got 15 points. The reason why China Coast Pidgin got 15 points is that the language declined so slowly. During the 19th century, Britain had traded with China through tea. Then Britain succeeded in growing tea in India. This success led Britain in a different direction. There was no need for the UK to come to Shanghai thereafter. At the same time, China's interests shifted from Britain to the Pacific Islands to get items such as sea cucumber and so on. This economic and social change eventually caused a language shift from China Coast Pidgin to Pacific Pidgin. It was observed in this chapter that the cline is important in explaining language decline. The same observation applies to contact languages outside Oceania. It should also be added that from this viewpoint, one may be able to predict risk for an endangered contact language.

5. Conclusion

Section I attempted to illustrate that the current linguistic situation in Papua New Guinea is different from that of Nauruan Pidgin in Nauru. The socio-historical backgrounds of Tok Pisin and Nauruan Pidgin relate to sugarcane and phosphate respectively. Section II surveyed linguistic features with special emphasis on Tok Pisin and Nauruan Pidgin. We see that the Tok Pisin does not correspond to Nauruan Pidgin in syntactic natures. Section III considered factors affecting contact language stability. The cline theory helps to explain the degree of language decline. Both geographical and socio-political factors may account for them. Especially political factors are some of the most influential in a cline. Section IV demonstrated the degree of stability by scoring each contact language both in and outside Oceania.

I have concluded that the cline showing language decline is a valid argument. Tok Pisin is one of the most stable contact languages, and Kanaka English unstable. Nauruan Pidgin is positioned in the middle of a continuum. Again, the cline is important in explaining language decline.

Note

1. Okamura (2003) argues the question of language decline. I developed the idea a little further here in the paper. I am indebted to Dr Jeff Siegel for his help in the research for this article while I was in the University of New England between 2000 and 2001. I would like to thank Mr Dicks Thomas (University of Papua New Guinea) for his valuable comments on Tok Pisin.

   I should also like to thank some members of Nauru-Tsuushinkai and Nauru-Yonkoukai in Japan for doing interviews, the Education Department in Nauru for arranging my interviews with the local people and the National Archives in Australia for providing important background information.

References

Clark, H. (1980) In search of Beach-la-Mar: Towards a history of Pacific Pidgin English. *Te Reo* 22, 3-64.

Demmke, A. et al. (1999) *Nauru population profile—A guide for planners and policy-makers*. Secretariat of the Pacific Community: Noumea, New Caledonia.

Franklin Karl J. (1968) *Tolai language course*. Department of Information and Extension Services.

Haarman, H. (1985) *Gengo seitaigaku* (Linguistic ecology) Tokyo: Taishuukan.

Hall, R. A. (1961) How Pidgin English has evolved, *New Scientist* 9, 413-415.

Hancock, I. (1971) A map and list of Pidgin and Creole languages. In Hymes (ed.) *Pidginization and Creolization of Languages*. Cambridge: University Press.

Mihalic, F. (1971) *The Jacaranda dictionary and grammar of Melanesian Pidgin*. Brisbane: Jacaranda Press.

Mühlhäusler, P. (1985) *The number of Pidgin Englishes in the Pacific. Papers in Pidgin and Creole Linguistics No.4*. Canberra: Australian National University.

Okamura, T. (1990) Sabujekuto maakaa ni tsuite (Subject referencing marker in Tok Pisin.). In: *Osaka Jogakuin Junior College Kiyo* 21: 165-194. (in Japanese)

Okamura, T. (1998) Oseania no gengo kongoo (Language mixing in Oceania). *Micronesia*, 30-38. Japan Institute for Pacific Studies. (in Japanese)

Okamura, T. (2003) Language mixing in Nauruan Pidgin. *Gengogaku Ronso*. Linguistic Circle of Okayama University.

Romaine, S. (1993) The decline of predicate marking in Tok Pisin. In: Francis Byrne and John Holm (eds.) *Atlantic Meets Pacific*, 251-260. Amsterdam: John Benjamins.

Siegel, J. (1990) Pidgin English in Nauru. In: *Journal of Pidgin and Creole Languages*,157-186. Amsterdam: John Benjamins Publishing Co.

Todd, L. (1984) *Modern Englishes: Pidgins and Creoles*. Oxford: Basil Blackwell.
Underwood, G. (1988) Accent and identity. In *Methods in Dialectology*, Maltilingual Matters.
Wurm, S. (1981) Pidgin languages, trade languages and lingue franche in Oceania and Australia. In S.A. Wurm and S. Hattori, (eds) *Language Atlas of the Pacific Area* part 1, map 24. Canberra: Australian Academy of the Humanities, in collaboration with the Japan Academy; *PL*, C-66.

The German Language in Papua New Guinea

Craig Alan Volker
Gifu Shotoku Gakuen University, Japan

1. The German colonial period

German influence (some would say meddling) in Melanesia dates from the 1860s, when planters and traders such as Johann Cesar Godeffroy & Sohn of Hamburg established copra plantations in what became known as the Bismarck Archipelago (Dotlan 2005), The actual German colonial administration of what became known as German New Guinea (Kaiser Wilhelmsland and the Bismarck Archipelago) began on 3 November 1884 with the proclamation of German sovereignty over 249,500 square kilometres of northern Melanesia and, in the following year, most of Micronesia (Anton n.d.). After German East Africa, this was the largest of the colonies of the pre-World War I German Empire. As was so often the case during European imperialism, German sovereignty was proclaimed in a foreign language, German, without the consent or even the knowledge of the sovereign indigenous peoples living there.

At first, German colonial administration was delegated to the Neuguinea-Compagnie, an actual colonial government not being formed until 1899 (Schnee 1920: 578). This brief attempt at creating a colonial empire ended with the outbreak of World War I, when Australia and Japan invaded and then occupied the parts of German New Guinea that eventually became the League of Nations mandated territories of New Guinea (under Australian administration) and

Micronesia (under Japanese administration), respectively.

Although German colonial rule was relatively short, the effects of German colonial rule can still be felt in contemporary Papua New Guinea. Disputes involving land alienated during the German colonial period flare up from time to time in the northern coastal and island provinces, much retail commerce in East New Britain and New Ireland is still in the hands of ethnic Chinese families whose ancestors were brought in as workers during the German period, and the Bulominski Highway in New Ireland, named for the German governor who had it built, is still one of the best highways in the nation. Even the spread of Tok Pisin as a lingua franca had its roots in the German period. The German language itself however, has left few lasting traces other than some geographic names and a relatively small number of loan words in Tok Pisin and some vernacular languages.

1.1. German in administration and education

When the Germans arrived in New Guinea, they found a lingua franca already in place, the Pidgin English that became Tok Pisin. As Keesing (1988) has shown, this language had its genesis in the sailing ships of the central Pacific with their multilingual Pacific Islander crews. When Melanesians were recruited, often by force or fraud by 'blackbirders', to work on plantations in Fiji, Queensland, and German Sāmoa, this pidgin became a lingua franca among workers and with outsiders, such as European employers and Chinese traders. When workers returned home, they brought knowledge of the pidgin with them and taught it to others.

Because a lingua franca already existed, there was no urgent drive on the part of plantation owners or other commercial interests to promote German as a language of wider communication. While German was, of course, spoken among the relatively small number of colonial administrators and other Germans in the colony and used in all government correspondence, there was some feeling that it was good to have a linguistic distance between the indigenous population and their 'masters'. Indeed, some went so far as to feel that the indigenous population should be denied access to German altogether so that the ruling European minority could have a 'secret language' (Mühlhäusler 1984: 35).

While the government position was not this extreme, only modest attempts were made to introduce education in German, in spite of public statements about the duty of a colonising power to promote European "civilisation" and to provide at least primary education (Schnee 1920: 308). In Germany itself, there was nationalistic interest in promoting German in all the colonies. In 1897, for example, the German Colonial Society lobbied the government to provide grants to missions following a government curriculum that encouraged learning German (Schnee 1920: 308). Mühlhäusler (1984: 34) reports that as World War I broke out, the colonial government was drafting legislation to embark on a significant expansion of German-language education in an effort to replace Tok Pisin with German. It never had the chance to enact this legislation.

Education was a responsibility overwhelmingly undertaken by the various missions in the colony. The *Deutsches Kolonial-Lexikon* mentions only two government schools in the colony, one in Rabaul (Simpsonhafen) and the other in Saipan, then a part of German New Guinea. In contrast to this paltry government involvement in education, it lists 56 Protestant and 189 Catholic schools, all at the primary or vocational school level. These schools sometimes taught in German, but more often used a local language or a vernacular that had been selected as a 'church lingua franca', such as Kâte or Jabem in Kaiser Wilhelmsland or Kuanua in the Bismarck Archipelago. Although as late as the 1970s, there were some individuals in Rabaul with a communicative command of German as a result of attending these schools (Volker 1982: 10), this was individual, not community, bilingualism.

There is no evidence that a true pidgin German developed in the colony. Mühlhäusler (1986: 35-36) gives examples of what he calls 'Pidgin German' written or spoken by New Guineans working at German mission stations, but there is so much variation in the data that these samples must be regarded as the poorly learned German typical of second language learners, rather than as any kind of systematic language for interethnic communication. The highly variable features typical of pidgins in his data, such as the lack of a copula and a lack of inflections, can be explained as second language learner transfer by speakers of Tok Pisin.

2. Rabaul Creole German

Although there is no evidence of any type of Pidgin German developing as a lingua franca in the colony, German New Guinea, however, did produce what seems to be the only attested case of a German-lexifier creole language (Mühlhäusler 1986: 36), Rabaul Creole German or Unserdeutsch ('Our German'), the language of the 'mixed-race'[2] community that developed around the Vunapope Catholic mission near Rabaul in East New Britain. Rabaul Creole German had its origin in the orphanage opened in 1898 by Catholic missionaries at Vunapope, outside of what was then Herbertshöhe (today Kokopo), the capital of German New Guinea on the Gazelle Peninsula of New Britain (then Neupommern) (Volker 1989b). The orphanage was opened specifically to educate children of indigenous, usually Tolai, mothers and fathers from Europe, Asia, and Micronesia. At first, the school served only abandoned children, who were often brought in by village leaders. With the Australian invasion at the beginning of World War I and the subsequent repatriation of German nationals at the end of the war, the number of students increased, as the majority of German men living in family situations with indigenous mothers left their children at the orphanage before being repatriated to Europe. Moreover, in a policy reminiscent of the kidnapping of the 'Stolen Generation' of Australian Aboriginal children, after establishing control of the German colony, the early Australian administration also often forcibly removed mixed-race children who remained with their indigenous mothers in local villages.

Some of the children would have been too young to speak any language when they arrived at the school. Others came to the school speaking a number of different languages. Many spoke Kuanua, the language of the Tolai. Others spoke other indigenous languages and/or smatterings of one of the several immigrant languages, such as Malay, Cantonese, Tagalog, Trukese, or German. Most of those old enough to speak had a reasonable knowledge of the early form of Tok Pisin. Indeed, when they came together in the orphanage dormitories, they may have been the first community of prepubescent children for whom Tok Pisin was the primary language. In the school, the language of instruction and communication with the German and Dutch teaching and other mission station staff was German, even after the Australian takeover of the colony. English was introduced as an academic subject after World War I, but did not become a language of instruction until after the school was reorganized after the end of World War II. By this time several generations had passed through the school, usually marrying each other.

After the upheavals and destruction of New Britain during the Japanese occupation in World War II, the community regrouped, with most people remaining on the Gazelle Peninsula. Because of the restrictive racial divisions of the time, most members of the community married each other; integration into white Australian society and emigration to Australia itself were not possible, and mixed-race persons were encouraged to remain separate from indigenous people around them.

American teaching missionaries were brought in so that the Vunapope school could be restarted as an English-speaking institution. German was used for increasingly fewer purposes in the Vunapope mission community, so that the younger members of the community grew up as trilingual as their parents, but in Rabaul Creole German, Tok Pisin, and English, not German. The Vunapope mixed-race community did retain a strong German identity, however, with some even referring to themselves as 'brown Germans' and to the German 'homeland' they had never seen as the *Vaterland*. German Christmas carols and food were important even to families who were not descended from Germans at all (Volker 1982: 12).

2.1 Genesis as a creole

When the Vunapope orphanage first opened, all three of the classic conditions for the establishment of a pidgin language mentioned by Hymes (1971) were present, namely contact among several different languages, with one, German, dominating, distinct boundaries between the languages, and, given the authoritarian pedagogical practices of the time, considerable social distance between the students and German-speaking staff. Nevertheless, since the students already had a common pidgin language at their disposal, Tok Pisin, the question remains as to why a new language was developed.

Inventing new ways of speaking, often intentionally chosen to infuriate an older generation, are, of course, a common phenomenon to youth around the world. Often, as with contemporary *Chilltaal* street language in the Netherlands, this can involve aspects of language mixing (Appel and Schoonen 2005). In at least one other instance in Papua New Guinea, the resulting youth register has been a relexified pidgin language (Volker 1989b). In the case of the Vunapope mixed-race community, there was the additional need for an ethnic identity, which in Melanesia is often marked linguistically. Rigid racial barriers prevented mixed-race persons from assimilating into other ethnic communities in the Gazelle Peninsula; as one older Rabaul Creole German speaker explained, "We were neither real Germans nor Kanakas. We needed our own language".

This feeling, together with the near-universal ability of youth to invent their own speech registers, means that Rabaul Creole German is best regarded as a cant, i.e., a language specifically created to exclude outsiders. Just as Laycock (1989) has described for Pitcairnese, Rabaul Creole German was created by persons who always had access to a European language, but who, because of their plural heritage and sense of historical uniqueness, felt a desire to express a separate ethnic identity from the mainstream community of European speakers of that language.

2.2 How creole is Rabaul Creole German?

The syntax and morphology of Rabaul Creole German have been described in some detail by Volker (1982 and 1989a). These descriptions show a number of features that are common among creole languages around the world. Moreover, these features are so different from their equivalents in Standard German that they must be regarded as quite different phenomena than those of the modified immigrant dialects spoken by bilingual German settlers and their descendants elsewhere. Most striking in the examples below is the complete lack of German subject-verb agreement morphology and case inflections.

Unlike Germanic languages, pidgin and creole languages often have serial verb constructions. Rabaul Creole German serial verbs are much like those in Tok Pisin:

(1) RCG Du holen Eimer komm.³
       you:SG fetch bucket come
    TP Yu kisim baket i kam
       you:SG fetch bucket PM come
    'Fetch the bucket.'

Rabaul Creole German also uses a Tok Pisin-like prepositional construction as the most common genitive construction:

(2) RCG Haus fi Tom
       house for Tom
    TP haus bilong Tom
       house of Tom
    'Tom's house'

As in many pidgins and creoles, 'for' (*fi*, from German *für*) is used as a complementiser:

(3) I bin am denken fi kaufen ein Ferd.
    I am PPT think for buy a horse
    'I'm thinking of buying a horse.'

Rabaul Creole German also shows several features that are not necessarily creole by nature, but which exist in Tok Pisin and Austronesian languages, but not German. Foremost among these is the differentiation between inclusive and exclusive first person plural pronouns (*yumi* and *mipela*, respectively, in Tok Pisin, and *uns* and *wir*, respectively in Rabaul Creole German).

Like Tok Pisin and most Austronesian languages, Rabaul Creole German places interrogatives in a sentence-final position, whereas they are usually fronted in German:

(4) Du   laufen geht wo
     you:SG run   go   where
     'Where are you running to?'

Whereas German uses morphological affixation and internal change to mark singular and plural, Rabaul Creole German, like Tok Pisin, uses a plural marker, *alle* (in German 'all'), which is cognate with the Tok Pisin plural marker *ol* (from English *all*):

(5) De   Chicken war   gestohlen bei alle Rascal.
     the chicken was   stolen   by   PL   criminal
     'The chicken was stolen by the criminals.'

As the preceding example shows, the passive construction, rare in pidgin and creole languages, is a calque of the English construction using *be*, immediately followed by a past participle, and *by* followed by the underlying subject, rather than the German passive construction using *warden* 'become', the preposition *von* 'of' followed by the underlying subject, and a sentence-final past participle. Another construction that seems to be modelled on English is a durative construction with *be* and a present participle, as in example (3) above.

Vestiges of German remain in the use of an inflected copula, rare in pidgins and creoles, and in much of the morphology of polysyllabic content words, such as *Deutschtum* 'Germanness' and *Hochzeit* 'honeymoon' (literally *hoch* 'high' + *Zeit* 'time'). These vestiges, together with the apparent borrowing of non-creole-like English constructions, give credence to the view expressed above that, like Pitcairnese, Rabaul Creole German is a cant, i.e., a deliberately invented language variety created to provide a means of ethnic identity among people who were both German and Melanesian. This explains why it lacks many of the typical creole-like features discussed by Bickerton (1981) in his examination of creoles with a genesis in traumatic slavery or indentured service plantation conditions.

2.3 Reasons for the decline and extinction of Rabaul Creole German

The number of Rabaul Creole German speakers was never very large. In 1913, near the end of German rule, the total number of mixed-race persons in all of the settlements of German New Guinea was only 281 (Schnee 1920: 315). Policies of strict racial segregation during the Australian administration helped to foster cohesion and in-group marriage in the small community.

As Independence approached, however, the community began to lose this cohesion. The abolition of the White Australia policy and the granting of Australian citizenship to previously stateless mixed-race persons in New Guinea meant that many could move to Port Moresby and Australia. At the same time, the relaxing of the colour bar brought about an increase in marriages outside the community, both with European Australians and indigenous Papua New Guineans. At Independence in 1975, most members of the community opted for Australian rather than Papua New Guinean citizenship, and within a few years, almost all had moved to Australia. By the turn of the century, only a few dozen members of the community still lived on the Gazelle Peninsula, and only a few elderly persons could speak Rabaul Creole German. Although family ties and nostalgia for the Gazelle Peninsula remain, Rabaul Creole German itself is not used for daily communication. It is likely to become a completely extinct language during the first quarter of the twenty-first century.

3. Lexical influence of German in Papua New Guinean languages

Although like Rabaul Creole German, the German language itself has almost entirely disappeared from Papua New Guinea, linguistic reminders of German colonial rule do remain in the German names of many prominent geographic names and in loan words of German origin in some Papua New Guinean languages.

3.1 Geographic names

An important enduring linguistic heritage of the German occupation of Papua New Guinea is geographic names, including the name of the highest mountain in the country, Mount Wilhelm. As was common among all European imperialists, the German colonialists gave their own names to settlements, geographic features, and islands. Usually this was in spite of a commonly used local name, but in some cases, such as in the name of a large mountain range or island, the indigenous people of the area did not travel widely enough to have their own name. Many of these names were changed when the Australian administration took over after World War I, but in some cases they are still used in modern independent Papua New Guinea. A list of the most prominent German geographic names is found in Appendix 1.

3.2 Loan words of German origin

German loan words can be found in both vernacular languages and in the main lingua franca of both colonial German New Guinea and modern Papua New Guinea, Tok Pisin. In the vernacular languages found in areas where German control was strong along the north-eastern coast of the New Guinea mainland ('Kaiser-Wilhelmsland') and the islands of the Bismarck Archipelago, German words were often adopted together with items introduced by the Germans. These included plant names such as *nanas* 'pineapple' in the Nalik language of New Ireland (from German *Ananas* 'pineapple'), names of introduced technology, such as *mesa* 'metal knife' in several Bougainville Island languages (from German *Messer* 'knife'), and religious terminology, such as *Satan* 'Satan' (German *Satan*) in many languages of the region. In many cases, the introduction of the word was either via Tok Pisin or reinforced by its introduction into Tok Pisin. For many, and probably most, speakers today, the German origin of these words is unknown.

Although derived from an English-lexifier South Pacific Pidgin English, Tok Pisin became established as the main lingua franca in northern New Guinea and the Bismarck Archipelago during the German colonial period, and so it is only natural that many words came into Tok Pisin from German. These include some of the most common and distinctive words used in modern Tok Pisin, such as *rausim* 'remove' (from German *raus* 'outside'), *popai(a)* 'miss the mark' (from German *vorbei* 'past'), and *gumi* 'rubber tyre' (from German *Gumi* 'rubber'). In addition, there are several Latin-based words used by the Roman Catholic church, which have German cognates, such as *pater* ('religious father/priest' in both German and Tok Pisin), with many words that have identical or close cognates in English and German, such as *haus* 'house' (German *Haus*) or *Katolik* 'Catholic' (German *Katholik*) is not possible to say which of the two is the sole source. Indeed, in most cases, it is probable that hearing the word from two sources reinforced the introduction of the terms in the early stages of Tok Pisin.

With increasing exposure to English, and a marked decrease in long-term German-speaking residents in Papua New Guinea, most German-derived words in Tok Pisin have been or are being replaced by English-derived terms. This is particularly true with technical terminology. Whereas once most carpentry terms were German-derived, for example, today words such as *hobel* 'plane' (German *Hobel*), *maisel* 'chisel' (German *Meissel*), and *sigmel* 'sawdust' (from German *Sägemehl*) have been replaced by English-derived *plen*, *sisal*, and *pipia bilong so* (literally 'rubbish of the saw') (see Mihalic 1971 for more examples from a time when both German- and English-derived forms were current). In many coastal areas, German-derived words, such as *beten* 'pray, prayer' (from German *beten* 'to pray') and *ananas* 'pineapple' (from German *Ananas* 'pineapple'), are used mainly by older speakers, with younger speakers preferring English-derived equivalents such as *prea* 'pray, prayer' and *painap* 'pineapple'. Most speakers of Tok Pisin in the Highlands, which were never under German colonial control, do not use many of these German-derived words at all.

An often quoted percentage of the Tok Pisin lexicon that is German-derived is 7% (e.g., Mühlhäusler 1986: 192). Given the decline in the use of many words of German origin in recent years, it is likely that this percentage is exaggerated. In the online Mihalic Tok Pisin Dictionary (Burton and Gesch n.d.), for example, only 2% of the entries made as of July 2005 were of definite German origin, with a further 5% of possible joint German and English origin. Nevertheless, it must be stressed that those German-derived words that do remain are often words such as *rausim* 'get out' that have high-frequency use.

4. German in Papua New Guinea today

The enduring influence of the German government and its colonial policies is not reflected in any real presence of the German language in Papua New Guinea today, other than in the surprising number of German geographic names that still remain (see Appendix 1). German is not taught at any school attended by Papua New Guineans, and even the Papua New Guinean Foreign Service does not feel a need to provide German language training for its diplomats.

There were once two schools operating after World War II which were German-medium, both primarily for the children of central European missionaries. During the Australian colonial administration and for some time after Papua New Guinean Independence in 1975, German Lutheran and Catholic missionaries and lay workers continued to play an important role in the educational and other activities of their respective churches. After World War II, a German primary school, the Kathrine Lehman Schule, was operated by the Lutheran Church in Wau, a former gold mining centre in the mountains of Morobe Province inland from Lae. A similar German-speaking school teaching grades five to nine was opened near Goroka, Eastern Highlands Province by the Swiss Evangelical Brotherhood Mission, which started missions in the Highlands and Sepik areas of Papua New Guinea in 1954. Both of these schools enrolled only children from German-speaking families, the vast majority of whom were affiliated with these or other missionary organisations. These schools did not enrol Papua New Guinean students.

After Papua New Guinean Independence in 1975, government policies strongly encouraged missions and companies to replace foreign workers with Papua New Guinean citizens. These localisation policies and a sharp increase in violent crime in the years since Independence made the pool of German-speaking families in Papua New Guinea much smaller. The Lutheran school closed in the mid-1990s. The Swiss Evangelical Brotherhood Mission school is still open, as the Mission has a policy to keep its school open as long as any of its workers are in the country with children. In 2005 there were, however, only ten pupils at the school, of whom only three were from the Swiss mission itself.

As neither of these mission schools enrolled Papua New Guinean students, neither had a direct impact on the use of German by indigenous Papua New Guineans. Since German is not taught at any of the six universities in Papua New Guinea, the only place where Papua New Guineans have had an opportunity to learn German formally since Independence was at the Lae International High School. This school has also been affected by the decline in the number of expatriate families. Because of the downsizing this imposed, German was dropped from the curriculum in 2003. At the time German classes were discontinued, about twenty students were studying German, about half of them Papua New Guinean.

There is little likelihood that German will again be taught in any school attended by Papua New Guineans. This does not, of course, mean that there is no demand by individual Papua New Guineans to learn the language. Students studying in central Europe do study the language formally in Europe, and there is the occasional desire to learn German formally or informally because of international marriage or other personal relationships. Nevertheless, given Papua New Guinea's position in the English-dominant Asia-Pacific region and the fluency of most educated central Europeans in English, there is little need for large numbers of twenty-first century Papua New Guineans to learn German. The position of German in Papua New Guinea today has therefore returned to the position it had before German imperialism imposed itself in Melanesia in 1884, the language of a few linguistically isolated foreign sojourners. It is no longer a language of Papua New Guinea.

Appendix 1
Major Geographic Names of German Origin

German name*	Modern name	Changed?
Adelbertgebirge	Adelbert Range (Madang Province)	no
Alexishafen	Alexishafen (Madang Province)	no
Berlinhafen	Aitape (East Sepik Province)	yes
Binnenhafen	Binnen Harbour (Madang Town)	no
Bismarckarchipel	Bismarck Archipelago	no
Bismarckgebirge	Bismarck Range (Eastern Highlands, Simbu, Madang Provinces)	no
Dallmannhafen	Vanimo (Sandaun Province)	yes
Finschhafen	Finschhafen (Morobe Province)	no
Finschküste	Rai Coast (Madang & Morobe Provinces)	yes
Französische Inseln	Vitu Islands	yes
Friedrich Wilhelmshafen	Madang	yes
Hansemannküste	Sepik coast, northern coast	yes
Hagenberg, Hagengebirge	Mt. Hagen	no
Hatzfeldhafen	Hatzfeldhaven (Madang Province)	no
Herbertshöhe	Kokopo (East New Britain)	yes
Kaiserin-Augustafluss	Sepik River	yes
Kaiser-Wilhelmsland	NE New Guinea mainland	yes
Konstantinhafen	Erimba (Madang Province)	yes
Neuhannover	New Hanover (also Lavongai) (New Ireland Province)	no
Neulauenburg, Neu-Lauenburg	Duke of York Islands (East New Britain Province)	yes
Neumecklenburg, Neu-Mecklenburg	New Ireland	yes
Neupommern, Neu-Pommern	New Britain	yes
Ottilienfluss	Ramu River	yes

Potsdamhafen	Gabun (?), (Madang Province, east of the mouth of the Ramu River)	yes
Preußen-Reede	Lae	yes
Sattelberg	Sattelberg (mountain in Morobe Province)	no
Schleinitzgebirge	Schleinitz Range (New Ireland)	no
Schouten-Inseln	Schouten Islands (East Sepik Province)	no
Schradergebirge	Schrader Range (Madang Province)	no
Seeadlerhafen	Lorengau (Manus Province)	yes
Simpsonhafen	Rabaul, Blanche Harbour	yes
St. Matthias-Inseln	St. Matthias Islands (New Ireland Province)	no
Stephansort	Bogadjim (Madang Province)	yes
Stoschberg	Suilik? (New Ireland Province)	yes
Varzinberg	Vunakokor (East New Britain)	yes
Weberhafen	Nonga (East New Britain)	yes
Wilhelmsberg	Mt. Wilhelm (tallest mountain in PNG)	no
Willaumezhalbinsel	Willaumez Peninsula (West New Britain)	no

German data from Dotlan (2005), Moran (2004), and Schnee (1920)

*Translations of German geographic terms:

Archipel = archipelago	Hafen = harbour	Küste = coast
Berg = mountain	Halbinsel = peninsula	Neu = new
Binnen = inner	Inseln = islands	Ort = place
Fluss = river	Kaiser = emperor	Preußen = Prussia
Französische = French	Kaiserin = empress	Reede = road
Gebirge = mountain range		

Appendix II
Examples of Rabaul Creole German (Unserdeutsch)

1. Genitive constructions:
   - (a) Haus fi Tom
     house for Tom
     'Tom's house'
   - (b) Mein Vater-s Haus
     my father-s house
     'my father's house'
   - (c) Diese Car de Tyre
     this car the tyre
     'this car's tyre'

2. Comparative / superlative:
   - (a) Maria is mehr klein denn Des.
     Maria is more small than Des
     'Maria is smaller than Des.'
   - (b) Diese is de größ-te
     this is the bigg-est
     'This is the biggest.'

3. Inclusive / exclusive 'we':
   - (a) Uns bis neben Salz-wasser.
     we:exclusive are next.to salt-water
     'We (but not you) are next to the ocean.'
   - (b) Wir alle geht Rabaul.
     we:inclusive: all go Rabaul
     'All of us, including you, are going to Rabaul.'

4. Word order with auxiliary verbs:
   I wird bleib zwei Woche in Lae.
   I will stay two week in Lae
   'I will stay two weeks in Lae.'

cf. Standard German:

Ich	werde	zwei	Wochen	in	Lae	bleiben.
I	will	two	weeks	in	Lae	stay

5. Serial verbs:

   (a)

Du	holen	diese	Eimer	komm!
you	fetch	this	bucket	come

     'Bring that bucket here.'

   (b)

Du	laufen	geht	wo?
you	run	go	where

     'Where are you running to?'

6. Durative verbs:

   (a)

Er	wollte	wissen	ob	Yvonne	is	am	gehen.
he	wanted	know	if	Yvonne	is	at	go

     'He wanted to know if Yvonne is going.'

   (b)

Nachher	de	Königin	war	de	ganze	Abend
afterwards	the	queen	was	the	entire	evening

am	denken	von	alle	Namen....
at	think	of	all	name

     'Afterwards the queen was thinking all night long of the names…'

7. Passive:

Sein	Schtoa	war	gefärbt	bei	ein	Chinesen
his	store	was	painted	by	a	Chinese

     'His store was painted by a Chinese.'

8. Complementiser *fi* 'for'

I	bin	am	denken	fi	kaufen	ein	Ferd.
I	am	at	think	for	buy	a	horse

     'I am thinking of buying a horse.'

Notes

1. I would like to express my appreciation to the many members of the Vunapope community who taught me about their people and the Rabaul Creole German language, in particular Veronica Käse, Theo Hartig, Paul Ah Ming, Leonard Ah Ming, Johann Schultz, Elsa Lündin, Elsa Hörler, Harry Hörler, Edith Wong, Rosemary Buchey, and Sister Anna Katrina. Sadly, many of these friends are no longer with us. I would also like to acknowledge the assistance of Marsha Milani for information about the current state of German education in Morobe Province and of Dora Siegenthaler for information about the Swiss school in Orobiga, Eastern Highlands Province. For any errors or omissions, *mea culpa*.

2. Although possibly considered pejorative elsewhere, 'mixed-race' is the common term used in Papua New Guinea for and by persons with multiethnic heritages. Because it is a term of self-identification and one that does not have negative connotations in a Papua New Guinean context, it is used here.

3. Rabaul Creole German was a completely oral language and not used in writing. Because the phonology differed only slightly from German, a modified German orthography is used here.

4. The following abbreviations have been used in linguistic examples:
   PL = plural
   PM = predicate marker
   PPT = present participle marker
   RCG = Rabaul Creole German
   SG = singular
   TP = Tok Pisin

References

Anfinger, P. (1947) Die Geheimsprachen auf den kleinen Inseln bei Madang in Neuguinea. *Anthropos* 37-40: 629-696.

Anton, R. (n.d.). *Deutsche Schutzgebiete – Die Kolonien des Deutschen Reiches*. http://www.deutsche-schutzgebiete.de/neuguinea.htm

Appel, R and Rob Schoonen. (2005) Street Language: a Multilingual Youth Register in the Netherlands. *Journal of Multilingual and Multicultural Development* Vol. 26, No. 2: 85-117.

Bickerton, D. (1981) *Roots of language*. Ann Arbor: Karoma.

Burton, J and P. Gesch (n.d.) *Revising the Mihalic Project*. http://coombs.anu.edu.au/SpecialProj/PNG/MIHALIC/Index.htm

Dotlan, G. (2005) *Frontline18: Die deutschen Kolonien - Neuguinea und die Inseln des Stillen Ozeans.* http://www.frontline18.com/history/326/ .

Hymes, D. (1971) *Pidginization and creolization of languages.* London: CUP.

Keesing, R. (1988) *Melanesian Pidgin and the Oceanic substrate.* Stanford: Stanford University Press.

Laycock, D. (1977) Special languages in parts of the New Guinea area. In: Stephen Wurm (ed.) *New Guinea Area languages and language study vol. III*, 133-155. Canberra: Australian National University Pacific Linguistics Series C-40.

Laycock, D. (1989) The status of Pitcairn-Norfolk: creole, dialect or cant? In Ulrich Ammon (ed.) *Status and function of languages and language varieties*, 608-629. Berlin: de Gruyter.

Mihalic, F. (1971) *The Jacaranda dictionary and grammar of Melanesian Pidgin.* Milton, Queensland: Jacaranda Press.

Moran, M. (2003) *Beyond the coral sea.* London: HarperCollins.

Mühlhäusler, P. (1984). Tracing the roots of Pidgin German, *Language and Communication*, Vol. 4, No 1: 27-57.

Mühlhäusler, P. (1986) *Pidgin & creole linguistics.* Language in Society 11. Oxford: Basil Blackwell..

Schnee, H (ed.) (1920) *Deutsches Kolonial-Lexikon.* Leipzig: Quelle und Meyer. (Digitalised by the Stadt- und Universitätsbibliothek Frankfurt a. Main at http://www.ub.bildarchiv-dkg.uni-frankfurt.de/dfg-projekt/bildprojekt/Lexikon/Impressum.htm)

Volker, C. (1982) An Introduction to Rabaul Creole German. M.Lit.St. thesis, University of Queensland.

Volker, C. (1989a) Rabaul Creole German syntax, *University of Hawai'i Working Papers in Linguistics*, Vol. 21, no. 1, January - June 1989.

Volker, C. (1989b) The relationship between traditional secret languages and two school-based pidgin languages in Papua New Guinea, *Horizons: Journal of Asia-Pacific Issues (East-West Center)*, Vol. 3: 19-24.

Volker, C. (1991) The birth and decline of Rabaul Creole German, *Language and Linguistics in Melanesia*, Vol. 22: 143-156.

Notes on Japanese Language Teaching in Papua New Guinea

Yasunori Kawazumi
University of Goroka

1. Introduction

Japanese language teaching (JLT) in Papua New Guinea started in Sogeri National High School in 1981, which is Sir Michael Somare's old school. Then it also started in the University of Papua New Guinea, St Ignasius High School and the University of Goroka in 2003.

To understand Japanese with different social environment and life style, it may fun because students can learn entirely new things. Papua New Guinea is one of developing countries however, all the Japanese learners there are different from those of in Asia and Europe. What is important seems to me that how we could keep learning in class and maintaining the purpose. Also the learners traits, cultures and customs are important factors for the understanding of Japanese.

The aim of learning is not only to heighten four Japanese skills (reading, writing, listening and speaking), but touch upon the different culture, thought, custom and sense of value. To learn Japanese is to know Japanese people and culture. This is an important sphere. We are concerned with the current situation of Japanese language teaching in Papua New Guinea.

2. Japanese language teaching at UOG

Goroka is about one hour from the capital city Port Moresby by airplane. It is located in the middle of the nation, and a town with a mountain 1,600 meters above sea level. The University of Goroka (UOG) is a four-year national university of education studies for training high school teachers.

It is three years since JLT started at UOG. The programme has been dispatched by Japan International Co-operation Agency. We have two semesters. Each semester consists of 14 weeks. Three classes a week from level 1 to 4 are offered. Students can be enrolled and get three credits as an optional subject in one semester. We need to restrict the numbers who can take Japanese classes. In addition to this, with only one Japanese staff member and a shortage of classrooms, it hard to put Japanese classes on the timetable.

Some original textbooks (*Let's Speak Japanese 1* and *2*) are made by the author for eighty hours training each. All the students can take Japanese classes with different grades and departments. First, students put compulsory subjects on the timetable, and then they put Japanese classes in the empty spaces. The more the students increase who can take Japanese, the harder it is for us to give guidance how the students could finish all the subjects. Classes should be done during lunch time and even after four o'clock. Under these circumstances some students have to give up taking Japanese classes because they do not have enough space on the timetable.

In addition to the above, we formed a Japan Club and encouraged them to register for this club activity.

3. Training, aims and methods

The aim of Japanese language teaching here in PNG is to speak Japanese. It might be very difficult for the students to brush up their Japanese language competence because there are only three classes provided a week. We cannot say we have enough time to teach even over level 2 classes, which are heavily restricted in numbers. I often ask students to teach themselves only 15 minutes a day. They submit the necessary tasks outside the class. Again, there are only three classes a week.

Then we review in class what we did last time. Some students give up learning Japanese because of the difficulty of the language. Therefore review exercises are a must for them. It is hard for us to control the speed in class, so what is important is how we can keep students interested. I often use Japanese movies, videos and recent magazines in class. Furthermore I invite students to my house to experience Japanese meals. Also, they can enjoy origami, songs and plays. There are some Japanese people visiting Goroka, so I ask them to come to my class and have some fun with my students.

In order to have variation in class, a variety of teaching materials (including audio-visual material) can be used, and several Japanese songs are introduced. Japanese classes should be enjoyable, otherwise the educational effect would not be expected. It does not matter whether or not we very often make mistakes. To get credit is important, but the most important thing is to have some fun in class.

The first step is to learn Japanese hiragana for one month. After that hiragana can be used in different domains like printed materials and on white boards. It takes a little while for them to be able to understand the Hiragana syllabary, but soon after that they can take exams using it.

Students should remember how they learned English. Japanese hiragana can be learned in the same way by singing a song. Teachers must perform in a successful way. Otherwise students feel embarrassed. In the first place, only /a, i, u, e, o/ has to be exercised. If it is repeated in a good manner, then the cue /ka/ is given by the teacher, and /ka, ki, ku, ke, ko/ together. The practice however, should not take longer. If it improves, finally we encourage and praise the students. The major purpose here is to recognize that Japanese is not so hard to learn, and is fun. If the students enjoy teaching themselves outside the class, we could say the first step is successful. It is not much fun to memorise Japanese words and expressions alone. For students it is much fun to learn foreign language singing a song and acquiring numbers in a rhythmic way. To learn foreign language is to memorise words and expressions. It is much better for the beginners to learn pleasantly. To speak a lot of Japanese makes students interested in language learning. Although it is important for us to know Japanese grammar, to speak Japanese fluently and comfortably should be focused on in learning.

Sociolinguistic knowledge helps students progress in their language competence. Japanese language teaching in PNG provides them with some knowledge of Japanese language and culture. Also, they could learn Japanese behaviour through Japanese learning. In some countries, strict attitudes and speech can be respected, others not. Ways of greeting in Japan are quite different from those in PNG, which is actually a surprising fact for PNG students. It is a must for us to learn cultural backgrounds in order to be able to be a good speaker in any language. Not understanding different cultural backgrounds causes troubles in communication.

Small quizzes and handouts matters are necessary to the understanding of Japanese. Also to understand at a functional level and acquire the correct use of the language are expected. Students must remember that they have opportunities to talk with Japanese people using Japanese language they acquired. General greetings should be done without misunderstanding. Furthermore, facial expressions and polite manners are important to learn.

It is said that non-verbal communication consists of 60 per cent of a conversation. Even if the sentence is grammatically correct, there may be some cases unacceptable. Non-verbal communication helps the students understand when they talk with the native speaker of Japanese.

My original book can usually be completed in a few months. Generally, it is considered that average Japanese staff members tend to feel relieved when the students exercised correctly. Before requesting the correct Japanese by using a limited vocabulary, expressions and sentence patterns, how they could speak in a good Japanese in a total sense should be focused upon.

There is no shortcut to learn foreign languages. To get Japanese resources in PNG is extremely hard, but they study Japanese very hard. It is considered that we have to look after the students from the viewpoints of the students. Without these attitudes, we would not be able to achieve our goal.

4. Japanese spoken by Papua New Guineans

There are not enough linguistic data on Japanese language spoken by the New Guineans during the second World War. Mühlhäusler, for instance, showed Somare's experience (2000: 29) at a school opened by the Japanese military during the occupation, but the story was so sketchy that we could not classify and analyse the language used. Also Mühlhäusler quoted Laycock (1977: 1041) to describe the possibility of pidginized Japanese, but again there was no discussion about it.

The aim of the paper is not to report the linguistic data during the occupation, so there is not any space for discussion. It is likely that the data are not pidginised variety but interlanguage as Okamura (2002) mentioned.

Let us return to the subject. Last year a general meeting among Japanese teachers who teach the language in PNG was held in Goroka. The main purpose was to study how the teaching is conducted in each school, and we staff members proposed that the textbook and syllabus be unified. However, we did not reach a conclusive decision. It is probably because some staff members are not well trained for teaching, preparing the material and so on. Furthermore, we do not have any transport between the places we were sent individually. Due to financial problems and regulations on JICA, all the staff members are not able to come together. The opportunity we could meet is once a year. Then we are not satisfied with the discussion. The current situation about teaching at UPNG, UOG, Sogeri and St Ignasius is almost the same, and we cannot afford to consider other schools. Under these circumstances, it is limited to consider error analysis, but we could discuss a few based on Japanese compositions and pronunciations collected in my class.

As far as Japanese pronunciation is concerned, there are mainly three problems. First of all, let us have a look at pronunciation. It seems that it is hard to distinguish choked sound from not choked (Number 1 below). Secondly, the distinction between /ha, ç, ɸ, he, ho/ and /a, i, u, e, o/ is confusing for Papua New Guineans (Number 2 below). Finally, they are very poor at pronouncing the long

/o/ vowel(Number 3 below).

1. The distinction between *kitte* (= stamp) and *kite* (= to come), *çitto* (= to hit) and *çito* (= person)

2. The loss of word initial sound, especially / ç / and /h/: *hikooki* (= aeroplane) becomes *ikooki*, *hai* (= yes) becomes *ai*, *hebi* (= snake) becomes *ebi*.

3. The shortning of long vowel: *soodesu* (=That's right.) becomes *sodesu*, *kuukoo* (= airport) becomes *kuuko*, *otoosan* (= father) becomes *otosan*.

The choked sound is one of special phonemes in Japanese, and it is constantly described as /Q/. It is counted as one syllable itself. Also it is characterized that it is not pronounced itself and it never occurs in word initial. Kubozono (1999: 27) produced his original textbook to practice the choked sound very well. This is true of other Japanese learners. The Japanese learners who come from Europe and America, for example, are not good at this distinction. (This observation is instructed by Okamura p.c.)

The loss of /h/ in word initial is not peculiar to Papua New Guineans. For example, Kashima (2002: 61) pointed out that the Japanese learners from the republic of Haiti often use 'Aichi' for 'Haichi' (= Haiti). Kashima mentions those who have no /h/ sound in their mother tongues have to pay special attention when using it.

The shortening of long vowel is not peculiar to Papua New Guineans as well. Japanese learners from all over the world often make this mistake.

Let us go on to the grammatical errors. The utterance No.4 below is the example of mistaking which vocabulary item to use. The error is caused by incorrect use of an English-Japanese dictionary. When looking up a dictionary for English word 'cold', we could get both *samui* and *tsumetai* as Japanese translation. *Samui* can be used in the context like *samui asa* (chilly morning). Then the distinction between *samui* and *tsumetai* becomes ambiguous.

Utterance 5 below is also the example mistook the choice of vocabularies. The English 'wear' has different meanings, i.e., it can be used when wearing shoes, dresses and eye-glasses. On the other hand, in Japanese we have each individual words for 'wear': '*haku*', '*kiru*' and '*kakeru*' respectively. This sort of correspondence between English and Japanese often causes errors.

The utterance No.6 below is understandable. When we have particular food like *gohan* (= rice) and *tsukemono* (= pickle), we have to use verb '*taberu*'. Then '*shokuji*' does not indicate particular food, but general term for food. In this case we must use the verb '*itadaku*'.

The utterances No.7 and No.8 are contrary to that of No.6. The *aisukuriimu* (= soft serve) and *deeto* (= date) both indicate a particular object, so '*kau*' and '*suru*' should be used.

4. a)   samui   koohii (= for tsumetai koohii)
       cold   coffee
       'iced coffee'

  b)   ureshii   jugyoo (= for tanoshii jugyoo)
       fun   class
       'a fun class'

  c)   majimena byooki (= for omoi byooki)
       serious   sick
       'serious sick'

5. a)   shatsu   wo   haku (= for shatsu wo kiru)
       T-shirt   OM   wear
       'wear a T-shirt'

  b)   kutsu   wo   kiru (= for kutsu wo haku)
       shoes   OM   wear
       'wear shoes'

6.   shokuji   wo   taberu (= shokuji wo itadaku)
       food   OM   eat
       'have some food'

7. aisukuriimu   wo   kaimono   suru (= aisukuriimu wo kau)
   soft serve   OM   shopping   do
   'get some soft serve'
8. deeto   wo   shinsee   suru (= deeto wo suru)
   date   OM   apply   do
   'have a date'
   OM= Object Marker

5. Overcoming a lot of difficulties in cultural differences

It is said that there is only 20 per cent people in PNG who can earn an income. The supply of electricity and water is limited to urban areas and suburbs. In villages, people are self-sufficient in food production. They can get money only from the market in town by selling vegetables grown in the village.

About 20 years ago, I was teaching at a senior high school in PNG. It is 20 years since I spent here in PNG for the first time. The everyday life in the village is almost the same as before. As far as JLT is concerned, it is not serious.

Classes last 50 minutes in the University. At the beginning of each semester, the difference between PNG TIME and JAPANESE TIME can be explained by the author. It is three years since I taught Japanese. Therefore eventually the expression JAPANESE TIME is spreading among the students.

To learn Japanese means to know Japanese culture. What is remarkable is some students learn Japanese very hard. I am very happy to have these students. It is good for them to learn about a different culture through Japanese. Some Papua New Guineans will like Japanese people and culture. This is a major target for me.

When learning a foreign language, people tend to think that it is important for us to learn useful and practical aspects. It seems to me that cultural studies other than language are much more important. We would find that there are some students who wish to succeed in Japanese proficiency tests and enter into Japanese universities or obtain an interpreter's license. We can make contact with a different culture, sense of value, and people through language studies. This gives us a key to understand each other.

First of all, we have to start constructing a reliable relation with the students. Then all the students are interested in the Japanese teacher, language and culture. Students ask us about Japanese religion, war, the atomic bomb in Hiroshima, wedding and divorce, family life and parents-children relation. To maintain interest and curiosity heighten the four Japanese skills. It is hoped that the students can grow to tolerate and encourage other cultures. Some Japanese visit Goroka each year. This is a good opportunity to talk with native speakers of Japanese. This makes the students excited.

6. Conclusion

It is only three years since Japanese language teaching at the University of Goroka started. There are many things to improve and arrange, but we find that the current situation of JLT at UOG has basically been successful as a first step. The characteristics of Japanese spoken by the Papua New Guineans are almost the same as in foreign countries. It is possible for the students and Japanese language teachers to overcome difficulties in cultural differences. Also, it is generally agreed that the financial problems and regulations on JICA should be improved.

References

Kashima, T. (2002) *Nihongo kyooiku wo mezasu hitonotameni: kiso kara manabu onseigaku.* (An Introduction to Phonetics: For those who studies with the aim of becoming a Japanese language teacher) Tokyo: Surii ee netto waaku. (in Japanese)

Kawazumi, Y. (n. d.) *Let's speak Japanese 1 and 2.* Unpublished.

Kubozono, H. (ed.) (1999) *Introduction to Japanese pronunciation: Theory and practice.* Tokyo: Kurosio. (in Japanese)

Laycock, D. (1977) Intrusive languages other than English: German and Japanese. In S.A. Wurm (ed.) *Man in the Pacific Islands.* Oxford: Clarendon Press. pp.1039-1044.

Mühlhäusler, P.& Rachel Trew (Translated by S. Asahi) (2000) Japanese language in the Pacific. *The Japanese Journal of Language in Society*, Vol.3 No.1 December 2000, pp.24-38.

Okamura, T. (2002) Japanese language teaching in Nauru during the occupation, *People and Culture in Oceania*, 18: 65-75.

Index

A
alternative constructions, 23, 26-27
Anton, R., 107
Appel, R., 112
appositional constructions, 23, 26-27
Austronesian languages, 77, 85, 90, 113

B
Bahasa-Indonesia, 63
Bahasa-Malaysia, 63
Baldauf, R., 57
Barbara, D., 59-60
Bickerton, D., 115
Bislama, 99, 101
Bougainville Island languages, 116
Bougainville, L., 41
Broken, 99, 101
Burton, J., 117

C
Cameroon Pidgin English, 97-98
Cantonese, 81, 91, 110
Chilltaal street language, 112
China (Chinese) Coast Pidgin, 81, 84, 94, 97, 102
Chinese, 92-94
Chinese Pidgin English, 82, 88, 92, 94, 97
Clarke, H., 94
cline, 77, 95-96, 99, 102-103
code switching, 72
colonial language, 64
contact language, 77, 95-98, 100-103
coordinate dependent clauses, 5-8, 12-15, 21
  constructions, 1, 6, 8, 12
  verbs, 4, 12, 15, 20, 22-23
coordinate independent clauses, 6-8, 13, 21
  constructions, 1, 5-6
Creole, 56, 77, 87, 89, 100, 110-115
Crowley, T., 56-57, 63
Cummins, J., 59

D
Demmke, A., 80
different-subject constructions, 14, 24
  referent, 14, 22
  suffix, 19-25, 27
dominant language, 59-60
Donohue, M., 2
Dotlan, G., 107
Dutch, 111

E
Eastern Highlands languages, 4
embedded constructions, 23, 25-27
endangered languages, 34-35
Enga, 2
Engan family, 1-2
English, 8, 36-39, 55-67, 69-73, 77, 79, 82, 91, 94-95, 98, 100, 111, 114, 117-119, 129, 132-133
error analysis, 131
European language, 77, 94, 112

F
Fearn, J., 79
Foley, W., 1-6, 15
Foster, D., 59
Franklin, K.J., 1-2, 7, 9, 12, 14, 27, 85-86, 89

G

Garasu, L., 40
geographical factors, 95, 96, 103
German, 37, 56, 77, 107-119
German identity, 111
Germanic languages, 112
German-lexifier creole language, 110
Gesch, P., 117
Gillian, A., 68
Gullah, 102

H

Haarman, H., 100-101
Hall, R., 94
Hancock, I., 94
Hernandes-Chavez, E., 59
Hindi, 63
Hiri Motu, 37, 55-58, 62-64, 66, 70-71, 73, 98
Holzknecht, S., 70
Hudson, R.A., 56, 72
Hughes, P.J., 60, 68, 70
Hymes, D., 111

I

interlanguage, 131

J

Jabem, 109
Japanese, 127-135
Japanese language teaching, 127-128, 134-135
JICA, 128, 131, 135
Johnson, R., 63
juxtaposed constructions, 24

K

Kale, J., 57

Kamene, S., 61, 65, 67
Kanaka English, 95-97, 101, 103
Kashima, T., 132
Kâte, 109
Keesing, R., 108
Kewa (pi), 1-6, 8, 12-13, 15, 19, 27
Kiwai, 2
koinization, 89
Krio, 102
Kriol, 97-98
Kuanua, 109-110
Kubozono, H., 132

L

Lang, A., 2
language attitude, 94
language decline, 33, 77, 82, 96-97, 102-103
language mixing, 90-91, 94, 112
language planning, 63-64
language policies, 55, 57, 59, 62-64
language right, 59
Lawes, G., 56
Laycock, D., 112, 131
linguistic diversity, 35, 49-51, 66
linguistic ecology model, 100
linguistic equality, 60
linguistic imperialism, 61
linguistic inequality, 68, 72
lingua franca, 55-58, 60-64, 66-67, 69, 71-73, 78, 98, 108-110, 116
Litteral, R., 36, 39, 40
loan words, 116
Longacre, R., 8
Lower Sepik-Ramu language family, 2
Luke, A., 57
Lynch, J., 56-57, 63, 70

M

MacGregor, W., 56
maintenance, 49, 58, 61, 96-97
Malay, 110
Maori Pidgin, 99, 101
Melanesian languages, 78, 114
Mihalic, F., 78, 117
minority languages, 59, 60
Miringka, R., 40, 45-46
mixed race, 110-112, 115
Mühlhäusler, P., 72, 94, 109-110, 117, 131

N

Nalik, 116
national language, 37, 62-63, 68, 78, 95, 101
Nauru language (Nauruan), 79, 87, 91-94
Nauruan-based Pidgin, 93
Nauruan Pidgin, 77, 80-82, 84-85, 87-89, 91-94, 96, 99-103
Nekitel, O., 61-63, 65, 67, 69
New Guinea languages, 5, 51, 115
Nichols, J., 4
Nigerian Pidgin English, 97-98
non-verbal communication, 130
Norfolk, 95-96, 99-101

O

official language, 35, 37, 56, 62-63, 66, 72, 95, 101
Okamura, T., 79, 81-82, 84-90, 92-93, 131-132

P

Pacific Pidgin English, 81-82, 86-91, 94, 102, 116
Palmer, M., 60
Papuan languages, 1, 6
Parker, N., 70
Pataki, L., 71

Payne, T., 8
Piau, J., 56-57, 63
Pidgin, 37, 42, 56-57, 77, 80-83, 85-89, 91, 93-94, 99, 108-109, 111-114, 116
Pidgin German, 109-110
pidginization, 88
Pijin, 99, 101
Pilipino, 63
Pitcairnese, 99, 101, 112, 114
Police Motu, 57
preservations, 33-37, 49-50

R

Rabaul Creole German, 110-115
relexified Pidgin language, 112
Roebuck, D., 60
Romaine, S., 79

S

same-subject constructions, 14
referent, 14, 17
referent, 14, 17
relation, 7, 17
suffix, 7, 15-17, 21
Schnee, H., 107, 109, 115
Scott, 4
secret language, 109
Shoonen, R., 112
Siegel, J., 82, 84, 88-89, 91-93
Siegruhn, A., 68
Skutnabb-Kangas, T., 59
Smolicz, J., 57, 59-60, 65
sociolinguistic diversity, 98-100
socio-political factors, 95-96, 103
Solomon Pidgin (Pijin), 90
Somare, M., 37, 63, 127, 131

stability, 77, 95-96, 99, 101-103
Standard German, 112
substratum influence, 85
Summer Institute of Linguistics, 39-40
Swahili, 63
switch-reference, 3-4, 8, 14, 19-24, 27

T
Tagalog, 63, 110
Teop, 47
Texas English, 99
Thirlwall, C., 60, 68, 70
Todd, L., 92
Tok Pisin, 55-58, 60, 62-64, 66-68, 70-73, 77-79, 82-86, 89-93, 98-99, 101-103, 108-114, 116-117
Tolai, 37, 77-79, 86, 89-90, 110
Trans New Guinea family, 1-2
Trans New Guinea languages, 1-4
Trukese, 110
Turner, M., 70

U
Underwood, G., 99
UNESCO, 34-36, 40, 49-51
Unserdeutsch, 110

V
vernacular literacy programmes, 33, 35-36, 38-42, 49
Volker, C., 109-112

W
Wurm, S., 1-2, 72, 94

Y
Yarapea, A., 7
Yimas, 4

Z
Znaniecki, F., 57

【編者紹介】

岡村徹（おかむら　とおる）

帝塚山学院大学准教授。
（専門　社会言語学）1961 年、福岡県に生まれる。九州大学大学院博士課程修了、博士（比較社会文化）。
〔主な業績〕[著書]『はじめてのビジン語―パプアニューギニアのことば―』（三修社 2005 年）、『オセアニアのことば・歴史』（渓水社 2006 年）［学位論文］「ナウル島の接触言語について―接触言語の安定度を決める要因―」（九州大学大学院比較社会文化学府 2004 年）、［論文］「ナウルビジンの保護」（『アジア英語研究』第 2 号 日本「アジア英語」学会 2000 年）

LANGUAGE IN PAPUA NEW GUINEA

発行	2007 年 10 月 20 日　初版 1 刷
定価	8000 円＋税
編者	©岡村　徹
発行者	松本　功
組版	iMat
印刷製本所	三美印刷株式会社
発行所	株式会社 ひつじ書房

〒112-0002 東京都文京区小石川 5-21-5
Tel.03-5684-6871 Fax.03-5684-6872
郵便振替 00120-8-142852
toiawase@hituzi.co.jp　http://www.hituzi.co.jp/

ISBN978-4-89476-353-1　C3087

造本には充分注意しておりますが、落丁・乱丁などがございましたら、小社かお買上げ書店におとりかえいたします．ご意見、ご感想など、小社までお寄せ下されば幸いです。